C000088711

Forensic Psychology

Connor Whiteley

Copyright © 2020 Connor Whiteley

All rights reserved.

ACKNOWLEDGMENTS

Thank you to all my readers for buying this book and supporting me as without you I couldn't do what I love.

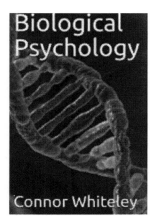

**GET FOR FREE
WHEN YOU
CLICK THE LINK
BELOW!**

https://www.subscribepage.com/n9v0d5

INTRODUCTION: WHAT IS FORENSIC PSYCHOLOGY?

Forensic Psychology is honestly one of my favourite types of psychology because I love the criminal mind and crime-related behaviour.

However, I must confer that forensic psychology is not profiling or what we typically see on television programmes. Such as CSI, NCIS or Bones.

In this chapter, we will be exploring what forensic psychology involves before we explore the various topics of forensic psychology.

What is Forensic Psychology?

This is a difficult question as there is no one answer.

Forensic psychology could be defined in many ways including:

- The psychological study of crime.
- The scientific behavioural study criminals.
- The science of studying crime-related behaviour.

I think we can all agree that these definitions are okay and do describe what we know as forensic psychology, but they are all wrong or not as good as they could be.

For example, the first definition states that we only study crime but forensic psychology studies more than crime.

The second definition has the same

problem as it states that we only study criminals.

Finally, the third definition is a bit ambiguous as forensic psychology does study crime-related incidents, but this definition possibly sounds as if forensic psychology studies everything but the crime itself.

Consequently, what is forensic psychology?

We can define forensic psychology as the activities of all psychologists whose work is related or contributes to the criminal justice system.

I know that this sounds complicated, but I'll explain it in the next section.

The Autonomy of Forensic Psychology

Is forensic psychology autonomous of other fields of psychology?

I ask you this question because other fields of psychology are quite autonomous, yet no subfield can be completely autonomous; as biological psychology is relatively autonomous as it studies biological processes and behaviour, so it doesn't draw very much information from other subfields. Like: cognitive psychology that focuses on mental processes.

The answer to the question is no.

Forensic psychology is not an autonomous subfield as psychological areas that are related to forensic psychology include but are not limited to:

- Social psychology- it's important to understand how the psychological processes within groups impact crime.
- Clinical psychology- it's important to understand as mental disorders impact or relate to criminal behaviour.
- Cognitive psychology- it's important to know how a person's mental processes can cause them to commit a crime.
- Developmental psychology- it's important to know how child development can cause crime.
- Personality- how a person's personality increases their likelihood to commit a crime.

Overall, as you can see forensic psychology works with and draws on the knowledge of other fields to help us understand crime and crime-related behaviour.

Forensic psychology as a field:

Forensic psychology is a very unique field within psychology as within most fields you can either be a researcher; so you research behaviour; or you can be a practitioner; where you apply the research to the real world in treatment or other settings; so you cannot be both.

However, in forensic psychology, you can be both.

This career opportunity is very interesting as there is often conflict between practitioners as well as researchers. As a result, the researchers do not write the reports or research in a practical way or a way that the practitioners can use. Making it very difficult to apply the research that could be extremely beneficial to offenders on treatment programmes in a treatment setting.

Overall, forensic psychology is an amalgamation of psychological work and practices.

In addition, forensic psychology is a fast-evolving area which holds many national and international conferences to keep everyone updated.

Some of these conferences include:

- The British Psychology Society Division of Forensic Psychology Annual Meeting
- International Association for Correctional and Forensic Psychology

Where can you work as a Forensic Psychologist?

Forensic psychology offers a lot of different work opportunities for you including:

- Treating offenders in a public or private prison
- Treating offenders in hospitals or other clinical settings
- Carrying out assessments on offenders. These assessments can possibly include suicide risk assessment and clinical assessments.
- Research- which is covered in the next section
- Consultancy

Even within the research side of forensic psychology, there are a lot of options for you.

For instance, you could research:

- Gangs- what causes them?
- Sexual aggression- why do some people commit sexual offenders and others do not?

- Firesetting- why are more males arsonists compared to females?
- Violence- what social causes provoke aggression?
- Child abuse- why abuse children?
- Terrorism- what causes terrorists to commit acts of mass murder?

All these areas of research involve both basic research; where you just research the fundamental variables, which is typically done in labs; and applied research. This is where you use the research in the real world.

Ethics within Forensic Psychology:

'Beware the actions of man.

Beware the lust for power and knowledge.

Beware the morality and ethics of a man'

-Connor Whiteley

Whilst I say that quote jokingly, it is no less true as ethics is a major part of psychology and the ethical guidelines were bought into creation by Man's questionable and *evil* actions as their lust for power as well as knowledge made them do harsh and unethical things to people.

For example: in the Stanford Prison Experiments in its oversimplified form where the researchers placed people in a situation without oversight to see what people would do as they wanted the knowledge to understand human behaviour further. Resulting in the unethical treatment of the people in the prisoner condition.

Please check out Sociocultural Psychology for more information.

Linking to forensic psychology, ethics can impact our ability to study criminal behaviour for a few reasons.

For example, we cannot study rape in a natural setting as this would be extremely unethical as we would effectively be watching a rapist rape a person and allowing it to happen for the sole purpose of gathering data. Whilst, the rape victim's life was destroyed.

That was one extreme example.

A less extreme example would be if researchers joined a gang and carried out drug deals (illegal behaviour) in order to gather data on drug users and the world of narcotics.

Therefore, as you can see ethics can inhibit forensic psychological research.

How can Forensic Psychology help the progression of Justice?

Forensic psychology can be extremely useful in the quest for justice, but with all disciplines. Forensic Psychology does have its limitations. This will be explored later in this book.

Some ways that Forensic Psychology can help the progression of justice include:

- It can improve eyewitness testimony.
- It can inform police procedure. For instance, by giving them more reliable ways to improve suspect identification.
- It can reveal what is involved in crime.
- It can inform treatments for offenders.

Attitudes and Philosophical Perspectives to have in Forensic Psychology:

Whilst, this section is more aimed at students of forensic psychology, I still strongly believe that this will be useful throughout this book as together we will have to be critical of research in Forensic Psychology.

Therefore, within Forensic Psychology (and wider psychology) it's important to bear the following in mind:

- You need to be analytical and critical.
- Don't use common sense has this causes too many problems and it often isn't correct.
- You should be sceptical but not cynical.
- You need to remember that crime has a context. For example, a mother killing the man who

slaughtered her daughter is different from a woman who killed her boyfriend because he was going to leave her. Despite them both being murders.

- You need to examine theories as well as beliefs scientifically.
- When you try to understand or explain a crime, you need to consider both situational factors; like a poor neighbour, abusive parents and having children; and individual factors. Like: intelligence and abnormal sexual arousal.

History of Forensic Psychology:

Forensic Psychology in the early 1900s had great interest before it died and picked up in the 1970s again.

However, Forensic Psychology can be traced back centuries as the concepts of insanity and fitness to stand trial are centuries old.

Forensic Psychology has developed an infrastructure to encourage its continued existence through international conferences, publications and journals.

Now that we have a basic understanding of what Forensic Psychology is, we can now start to explore the various topics within Forensic Psychology in more depth...

CHAPTER 1: DEVELOPMENT OF OFFENDING: THEORIES AND PRESPECTIVES

Why do criminals offend?

That will be our focus in this chapter.

There are many theories about why people offend. Resulting in these theories being put into categories.

For example:

- Individual- these theories focus on the reasons for offending at an individual level.

- Group- these theories focus on the offending at the social group level.
- Community influence- these focus on different areas that provide people with different opportunities to commit crimes.
- Societal and macro levels- these theories state that society is constructed in a way that creates crime.

Then these categories can be further broken down into different perspective despite these categories being perspectives in themselves.

- Individual
- Genetic
- History
- Deviant
- Focuses on individual
- Groups and socialisation theories

All perspectives are useful but hard to part them together to form one holistic theory of offending.

Theories of offending:

Now that we've covered the different perspectives that a researcher can take in order to investigate why offending occurs. We can begin to look at some theories.

Social Learning Theory:

This theory states that we learn by observing others and their consequences in its simplest form.

For more information, please check out Sociocultural Psychology by Connor Whiteley.

As a part of Social Learning Theory, Bandura, Ross and Ross (1963) state that having a model is important to learn behaviour from.

For example, we learn directly from family and friends.

In addition, reinforcers work well with this theory as reinforcers can be used to show that the watched behaviour is good.

Examples of reinforcers include:

- Sex
- Social acceptance
- Money
- Social approvals

Linking to offending:

Social Learning Theory can be used to explain offending because the theory states if a child; for instance; watches their brothers or sisters commit crimes without receiving negative consequences. Then the child will learn that this is acceptable and wish to copy it.

This desire to copy the behaviour is even stronger when a reinforcer is involved.

Such as: if the parents were giving the brothers and sisters money for stealing, or even something as simple as love.

Evaluation of Social Learning Theory as an offending theory:

Whilst, social learning is useful as it explains the processes of learning complex behaviour and how it links to offending as well as there is no need to assume the offender has a pathology.

The theory doesn't explain what conditions are needed for people to learn criminality.

In case, you're confused about the

negative of Social learning as I'll use an example.

The example I've used is for all intents and purposes made up where I have just applied what social learning theory states and I've applied it to offended.

Nowhere in the original study or theory does it outline criminality.

Cognitive theories of crimes:

Throughout this series, I hope that I have shown you the power of mental processes also known as cognition as it applies to memory, mental disorders, health and more.

For that reason, it wouldn't be right if I didn't include cognitive psychology in this book.

Intelligence:

Whenever people see a criminal many of them think that the criminal has low intelligence and that's the reason why they committed the crime.

Yet I will ask you the following questions…

Do white-collar criminals have low intelligence?

Do world leaders who commit crimes have low intelligence?

Does a doctor who is a criminal have low intelligence?

Overall, I hope that those questions begin to help you to understand that criminals don't always have low levels of intelligence.

In fact, most of the time criminals have average or high levels of intelligence.

However, the general theory of intelligence is that having a lower IQ means that you have poorer marketable skills leading to an increased risk of unemployment. Leading to a poor ability to avoid risks as you need money to survive so you get caught easier as you don't have the intelligence to avoid getting caught.

Overall, this theory is a controversial hypothesis with weak support and a weak correlation with crime.

Self-regulation and risk behaviour:

Another cognitive theory of offending is that a lack of self-regulation and an increase in risky behaviour leads to offending.

Self-regulation is the ability to control your own behaviour and some research links low self-regulation with aggression as well as self-regulation is a limited resource.

Therefore, the theory states that if you use up your self-regulation and have a decreased amount of it then you may be more likely to commit inappropriate or criminal behaviour.

Though, whether self-regulation is a limited resource is still being debated.

Biological theories of crime:

Our biology can influence many factors that relate to human behaviour as explained in my Biological Psychology book.

As a result, some crimes could be biology-related.

Although, it must be noted all behaviours and crimes have biological and environmental causes.

One example of this is aggression-based crimes as testosterone can impact aggression levels.

Furthermore, Forsman and Langstorm (2012) suggested that genetics could play a role in adult violence across generations.

Thus, when combined with the fact that the inheritability of aggression is about 50%. It makes a good case for a biological cause for aggression.

On the other hand, servals genes are involved in aggression probably through the production of neurotransmitters and hormones, so testosterone isn't the only factor in aggression.

Overall, the theory suggests that testosterone causes offending because the testosterone causes aggression levels to increase. Making a person more likely to become aggressive and commit a violent crime.

For more information on aggression please check out Sociocultural Psychology by Connor Whiteley.

Biosocial theory of crime:

Personally, I love this theory as it's holistic, so it doesn't reduce the cause of a behaviour down to one singular cause.

However, as this theory is very long and detailed. We won't go into too much depth.

This theory was proposed by Eysenck as well as it combines both biological causes and environmental causes to produce a criminal act.

In more detail, the theory states that biological factors have a big impact, but that impact depends on external factors to various degrees.

Evaluation of the Biosocial Theory:

Whilst, the theory has good scope. It's far too broad and it cannot explain many aspects of crimes.

Theories of Violent offending:

When it comes to violent offending, biological theories get a lot of criticism as most violence is instrumental.

Basically, we learn violence by observing others.

Equally, when we try to categorise types of violent offenders, we encounter problems as typologies assume that people stick to one type. When offenders could show characteristics of many types.

Do violent video games increase aggression?

The idea behind violent video games increasing aggression is that the player practices and repeats the violent behaviour.

Leading to the reinforcement of the behaviour because it makes you feel good and the repetition leads to you developing a mental script of the behaviour. Meaning that you know how you're meant to act in a certain context. In this case, the context is violence.

Moreover, you become more desensitised to violence and aggression as the video game exposures you to violence more.

Overall, you repeat the violence, develop a mental script so you know how to be violent and you become desensitised so in the real world you are less inhibited and you know exactly what to do.

For instance: you know how to beat someone to death, and you know how to shoot up a school. Due to you have learned how to shoot guns in games.

Reality check:

However, this effect seems to be small.

Equally, the effect may be small but think about the millions that play violent video games, even if this effect is small.

It will still affect thousands of people.

Ultimately, it is probably a combination of things that leads to an increase in violence and not only video games.

Theories of sexual harassment:

Sociocultural theory:
This theory focuses on the social and political context that sexual harassment is created and occurs in. Additionally, this theory states that sexual harassment results from the society's sexism, inequity beliefs and attitudes.

Meaning that if a culture or society has a lot of sexism attitudes and gender inequities than sexual harassment is likely to occur.

A positive of this theory is that it's a logical synthesis of society's inequity, patriarchy and dominance.

A negative of the theory is that it's too broad and it doesn't go into detail. For example, the theory doesn't elaborate on what political and social factors can increase sexual harassment behaviour.

Organisational theory:

This theory states that sexual harassment is caused by a wide variety of organisational- related issues. Such as gender inequality and power, as well as sexual harassment is committed by peers or even subordinates to decrease the power difference.

Additionally, the theory plays a vital role in the focus on decreasing sexual harassment in the workplace.

An advantage of the theory is that it's supported by empirical evidence and tested as well as it links organisational factors together.

However, it doesn't account for individual differences.

<u>Sex role spillover theory:</u>
This theory brings together situational and individual characteristics whilst stating that people bring their own beliefs into the workplace and this

causes conflict. Ultimately leading to sexual harassment.

A positive of the theory is that it is a more holistic approach.

Although, the theory needs refinement and it focuses too much on men. This is a problem as women can commit sexual harassment as well.

Biological theory:
This is an extension of natural selection as men have a drive to reproduce as much as possible and there's a difference between men and women's reproduction strategies, so this leads to conflict.

An advantage of the theory is that it unifies evolution and sexual offending.

However, this theory is reductionist as it ignores cognitive and social factors that can play a role in sexual harassment.

Finally, this theory almost offers an excuse to people who sexually harass by saying that it's their biology, so it is not their fault. These sorts of ideas are very dangerous.

Four-factor theory:
(O'Hare and O'Donohue 1998)

This theory believes that four factors must be overcome/ maintained to perform the behaviour.

The four factors are:
· Motivated to harass
· Overcome internal inhibitions (mortality)
· Overcome external inhibition (professionals)
· Overcome victim's resistance
A positive of the theory is that it is holistic and explains sexual harassment in-depth, but it's not fully tested and

factors 1 and 2 have not been researched.

Neuropsychological approach to theories of offending:

This approach focuses on the brain and any brain abnormalities in the brain.

The results for this research are very mixed as sometimes there are abnormalities in the brain of offenders and sometimes there aren't.

Plus, it's correlational so it's possible that the abnormalities caused crime, or the crime caused the abnormalities.

As in correlational research, you can only see if there's a relationship between the brains of people and those people committing crimes.

Evaluation of the neuropsychological approach to offending:

A positive of this approach is that knowledge of neuropsychology could lead to better treatment as we would have a better understanding of how the criminal brain works. Therefore, we can deliver targeted treatment to 'fix' these brain abnormalities.

On the other hand, we are still a long way from fully understanding the neuropsychology of criminals.

Addiction:

Could addiction be responsible for crime?

Could a criminal be addicted to crime?

When I first came across this addiction reason for offending, I was interested because I had become interested in the wider application of addiction when I wrote my Health Psychology book. That said that our addiction to fat and sugar causes obesity.

Consequently, I was interested to apply the process of addiction to crime.

In short, addiction works in the following way:

- You do something that causes your brain to feel dopamine and other neurotransmitters and hormones.
- These make you feel amazing.
- Then you continue to do the behaviour, so your brain continues to release these neurochemicals.
- But over time your brain builds up a tolerance to these neurochemicals.

- Meaning that you need to do the behaviour more to get the same effect.

Now that we know the basics, let's apply it to crime using a theft example.

- A thief steals a piece of jewellery without getting caught.
- Then the brain release neurochemicals as a reward.
- Making the thief feel great.
- Making the thief steal more to get the same rush.
- However, over time their brain starts to build up a tolerance.
- Resulting in the thief stealing a lot more and possibly committing higher stake thefts to get the same rush.

Evaluation of the addiction theory of offending:

A positive of the theory is that it could explain why repeat offenders commit crimes.

Although without more research we do not know if addiction is a general trend or something that only happens to a select few.

For more information on addiction please check out Health Psychology by Connor Whiteley.

Childhood offending:

Children offend for many different reasons.

Children committing crimes is a hard truth, but it happens.

But why does it?

But why do children commit crimes when society desires them to have a safe, happy, crime-free childhood?

That will be the focus of this section.

Personal anecdote:

Before, we get into the psychology of childhood offending. Let me tell you a personal experience I have had with childhood offending.

Note: I was NOT the offender.

I used to have a best friend who was a great person and… it's hard to put into words how great of a friend he was.

Nevertheless, he used to be a lookout for his brothers as they robbed houses.

Moving into the psychology of that incident, I strongly believe that multiple factors were involved in him committing the criminal act because he was an accomplice in the crime.

I believe that it was peer pressure, social approval and other factors that lead my friend to commit these childhood crimes because my committing these crimes his brothers would approve of him and he did say to me before that he was picked on by his brothers.

Therefore, it's reasonable to assume that to get his brothers to stop picking on him. He would commit these crimes.

Reasons for childhood offending:

There are many reasons why children commit offences and all the following are risk factors that increase the likelihood of offending.

- More extreme punitive ways to raise a child
- Lack of supervision
- Family disruptions

- Deviant parents
- Lack of love or rejection
- Parent's criminal behaviour
- Laxness
- Punitive parenting style
- Family disruptions and many more...

Protective factors:

In addition, to risk factors that increase the likelihood of childhood offending. You have protective factors that decrease the likelihood of offending.

These include:

- Stable relationships
- Supportive educational climate
- Supportive social network (not just family)

Losel and Blisener (1994) found that their resistant group had more protective factors than the deviant group.

In other words, the researchers found that the reason why one group was more resistant to offending than the other was that this resistant group had more protective factors.

Researching childhood offending:

When it comes to research, there are two main ways to study why some children offend and why others do not.

The first way is by comparing an offending sample with a non-offending sample- so you can see if there are any factors cause your offending sample to offend but not the other sample.

Secondly, you can study children who should theoretically offend due to life circumstances but do not offend.

Overall, I hope that you can now begin

to understand why people offend and the wide range of theories that exist to explain this criminal behaviour.

Part 1: Public, Victims and Crime:

CHAPTER 2: VICTIMS AND FEAR OF CRIME

Victims and fear of crimes:

Public and crime are honestly one of my favourite topics in forensic psychology because I love to learn how flawed the public's knowledge is and the impacts that has on the Criminal Justice System. Hence, why that will be our focus for this chapter.

Firstly, the path from committing the crime to punishment is very complex and it must be remembered that crime is a social problem as well.

To emphasize the complexity of the process from committing a crime to punishment. Here are the stages of crime. (Ainsworth, 2000)

- Will the victim notice crime?
- Will the victim report crime?
- Will the police record the crime?
- Will the offender caught?
- Will the offender be prosecuted?
- Will the perpetrator be found guilty?
- Will the perpetrator be sentenced?

As you can see, the path to punishment isn't straight forward as the case can be dropped or no undetected at any point.

Public and crime:

In addition to the crime being a social problem, crime is a public issue. Meaning that public opinion affects the justice system. Therefore, public concern needs to understand as it may affect how justice is delivered.

However, the public's perception of rates of crime is often inaccurate. (Ainsworth and Moss, 20002) and it's unrealistic to expect the public to have accurate perceptions. (Howitt, 1992, 1986)

The public's perception of crime is that society is becoming increasingly criminal and risky. (Doherty, 1990)

Whereas in reality, crime rates have been decreasing throughout history, but recently certain types of crime are on the rise.

Meaning that the public's perception is wrong.

<u>Fear of crime:</u>

Let's face it, the public fear crime and becoming victims of crime.

As a result of this fear of crime,

politicians and others use this fear in political contexts to gain favour and governments may actively try to influence it.

The reason for this influencing and political interest is because if there's less fear then the government is doing a perceived better job of tackling crime.

In other words, this is another example of politicians telling the public half-truths in an effort to gain favour and stay in power.

Where does the fear of crime come from?

There are many different sources of this fear. Such as Mass media plays a big role as they focus on the most serious of crimes. Meaning that you think that these major crimes are happening more often than they naturally occur.

Another example is direct knowledge of crimes were a crime has affected us directly and we have learned from that experience. For example, a crime in our community, a crime against a family member or even a crime against ourselves.

Finally, there are aspects of our personality and social characteristics that make us more likely to be fearful of crime.

For example, Bazzargan (1994) found that feeling lonely, having a poor education, believing that your neighbours are untrustworthy and having a lack of vigilance increased the likelihood in you becoming fearful of crime.

Fear-victimisation paradox (Clark, 2004)

That fact shows that being fearful of

crime is somewhat unneeded as this paradox shows that there are no relationships between rates of crimes and victimisation.

Here's an example, women are more fearful of crime than men. (Stanko, 1995) but men are actually most at risk of attack by a stranger.

Hence, demonstrating how being fearful of crime doesn't always mean that you will become a victim of crime.

Crime phobia (Clark, 2004)

Many people who are fearful of crimes say that they have a phobia. I know that this is what some of my older family has said as they can be very fearful at times about crime. Especially, after a terror attack.

However, the research suggests that the fear of crime isn't like a phobia because the fear of crime isn't dysfunctional or irrational.

Media bias:

In my opinion, this idea of media bias is one of the most important topics in Forensic Psychology because media bias; as you will see throughout the book; is linked with a lot of public knowledge.

As we use the media to learn about crime and other matters.

For example, if an individual has limited or very little opportunities to interact with a specific stereotyped group, then the individual will rely on the media's portrayed of that group in order to learn more. (Sanghana & Wilson, 2006)

Furthermore, Media interest regarding crime and in particular sexual offending has grown dramatically (Quinn et al,

2000)

However, reported levels of sexual assault have remained constant over the years.

This is an example of the public believing that sex offending is increasing but in reality, it isn't and the media is manipulating the public to believe in such ideas.

Finally, the media only likes to report sensational crimes.

Public opinion and Experts:

We will build upon this topic more in our next chapter but ideally, public opinion and experts need to appreciate each other and co-exist.

However, with the government choosing to do 'top of the head' polls instead of deliberation polls for political gain then the government only gets a skewed version of public opinion. That they use for political gain and not the benefit of the people.

CHAPTER 3: THEORIES OF THE FEAR OF CRIME

As always psychology loves a good theory and fear of crime is no exception as there are a lot of theories to help explain this fear.

Cultivation theory, (Gerbner, 1972)

This theory states that the fear of crime is caused by the consumption of mass media and its televisions that are used as a means of cultural transmission and it's this transmission of horrific crimes that creates the fear.

A positive of the theory is that other

research shows that people who watch more media tend to have higher levels of fear.

Nonetheless, this relationship is statistically weak, and the types of neighbourhoods and demographics of the sample weaken relationships even more.

Availability Heuristic theory (Shurun, 1996)

The availability heuristic refers to the extent to which the media creates vivid and accessible images of crime in people's mind. Making you feel unsafe if you enter a similar situation. Due to you remember a crime that is related to a situation like what you're currently in.

For instance, in see you a horrific murder in a dark alley and then you are walking down a dark alley later that night, then it's likely you will become fearful as you remember those images and fear that the same crime would happen to you.

A positive of this theory is that there is some supporting research, but I believe that it's too reductionist as it only focuses on a singular cause.

Cognitive theory (Winkel, 1998)

Our last theory for the fear of crime is a cognitive theory that proposes that the fear is a product of risk seriousness.

In order to find out the risk seriousness of the situation you times the subjective risk of being a victim with the perceived negative impact; this is the belief you have about the seriousness of the consequences of the crime.

Let's use an example because I know that this isn't the simplest theory to explain. For example, let's say that I think that the risk of me becoming a victim of a stabbing is 80% and I believe that the consequences of being stabbed are extremely serious. Giving me a score of 100%.

Therefore, to give me a product of risk and my fear of crime. I would calculate $0.8*1= 0.8$ or 80%. Meaning that I would have a high risk of being fearful of crime.

Additionally, I used very high numbers in my example to show that people's perception is flawed because this is there subjective opinion.

Whilst, there is evidence to support this theory, some evidence proposes that some people are more affected by victimisation.

CHAPTER 4: VICTMINOLOGY, RESTORATIVE JUSTICE AND PTSD

Victimology:

This area of psychology focuses on the victim-offender interface and it originally focused on victim characteristics that increase the likelihood of victimisation.

Yet now it focuses on how psychology can help victims to recover from their horrific experiences.

Victim decision making:

When it comes to reporting a crime, victims are central because it is the victims that bring the crimes to the justice system to be tried and prosecuted.

In fact, in the USA 3/5 of all crimes are reported by victims. Hence, showing how important they are in the system.

Although, there are many factors to consider when the victim is deciding whether to report the crime. For example, victims talk to others about victimisation and the impacts that this will have on them as well as they talk to other victims to get advice as they have been through the process before.

In addition, it depends on the type of crime that has been committed as people are more likely to report a murder than a minor theft.

Overall, when it comes to deciding whether or not to report a crime. The victim is completely a cost/benefit analysis. As I'll discuss later, sometimes the Criminal Justice System makes you a lot worse off.

Although, it is important to remember that the people who are targeted by crimes aren't the only victims. As a result of the friends, family and others can become victims of the criminal act themselves, as they try to support the victim a full understanding of how themselves are feeling.

This is because the indirect victims can become fearful of crime, they can despair as well as powerless, they can feel like the world will end and they can have survivor guilt.

Hence, demonstrating how criminal acts can have a ripple effect of sorts as they create victims.

Secondary victimisation:

Building upon what I briefly mentioned earlier, secondary victimisation is when you're victimised again by the justice system.

This secondary victimisation can occur because of the long examination that can prolong trauma, being embarrassed about events, having to give testimony that's a long process and feeling like the defensive team is personally attacking you.

To demonstrate this further let's use an example of a rape victim; I will not be going to graphic details.

This secondary victimisation can happen to a rape victim because the victims can feel embarrassed to be raped as well as lawyers can very burial when it comes to questions about the act that they suffered. Leading to secondary victimisation.

In addition, the rape victim is sadly going to be given trouble by society because there are a lot of social beliefs that can be extremely damaging to people. For example, it's murder victim lifestyle's that caused their death and the girl was asking to be raped.

Consequently, I think the thing to take away here is that we need to support victims better as well as question these social beliefs.

Vicarious victimisation:

This type of victimisation is very interesting to me personally as I want to become a Doctor of clinical psychology one day.

This type of victimisation is where police officers and other professionals become victims of the crimes because they are exposed to victims and horrors of the crime.

Some of the risk factors include: (Lewin and Greisberg)

- The person having a prior history of trauma
- The officer or therapist has a lengthy exposure
- Lack of work support
- Lack of supervision

These are some of the reactions that therapists have to work with victims: (Campbell, 1994)

- The therapists can become emotionally overwhelmed
- They can adopt the role of rescue
- Loss of belief in the effectiveness of the intervention
- Survivor's guilt
- Mirroring victim's emotions of rage, despair and terror.

Consequently, supervision and support

are important for professional. To help prevent this victimisation from happening.

Restorative justice:

Personally, I find this type of justice very unusually because restorative justice focuses on the imposed punishment of the offender by CJS as well as it focuses on repairing harm done by criminal activity through the cooperation of all parties.

In addition, everyone who was harmed even indirectly is the focus of this justice with healing and re-integration being the main objective.

Of course, this type of justice wouldn't be suitable for everyone like rape victims but reports say that this type of justice has shown good results at helping people move on after these dreadful criminal acts.

Outcomes:

Restorative Justice has a number of positive outcomes. Including the victim is satisfied, the offender feels like they've been treated fairly as they can explain their actions, as well as the mediation between the offender and victim, identify factors that led to the crime. Making it easier to understand and prevent in the future.

Examples of restorative justice:

Here are some examples of restorative Justice:

- Repartition
- Restitution
- Mediation
- Victim-offender mediation programme- research suggests a high satisfaction rate.

- Conference programme- this is similar to the example above but extend to family, police and more, and has positive outcomes with juvenile offenders.

Other strategies include circles, community service and ex-offender assistance.

PTSD:

Post-Traumatic Stress Disorder is a horrific disorder to have and it's the psychological consequences of victimisation.

Where you relive traumatic events and you typically avoid anything that reminds that trauma as well as you have severe anxiety which disrupts day to day life.

According to the DSM-5 (See Abnormal Psychology for more Information) this is the diagnostic criteria for PTSD:

Stressor:

In order to be diagnosed with PTSD, you need a stressor. Which can be witnessing an event in person, direct exposure or indirect exposure. Like hearing about it from a friend.

Intrusion symptoms:

When you have PTSD, you have nightmares of the event, intrusive memories as well as intrude, prolonged distress caused by reliving the traumatic event.

Theories of PTSD:

Stress-reponse theory (Horowrite, 1986)

This theory proposes that the trauma disturbs the victim's beliefs and the cognition before and after the event was very different.

PTSD is equally a defensive mechanism; avoiding memories of the event, and a healing mechanism as it provides you with an opportunity for you to work with the memories.

Personally, I love this theory because I love the idea that this could be a healing mechanism. After all, that would be reasonable. Considering that the memories keep showing up. Possibly giving you time to see them and think about them.

Other theories:

Pollock (1999) raised a question about can an offender suffer from PTSD as there are two potential links. Which are, suffers of PTSD can act more violently like some offenders do as well as an offender of a horrific crime can't cope with their actions, so they develop PTSD.

Berwin, Andrews and Valentine (2000) suggested that having a good working memory is important for stopping intrusion flashbacks.

Ono, Devtly and Shum (2016) carried out a meta-analysis on 25 studies on over general memory and found a strong associated between over general memory and PTSD.

Please check out Cognitive Psychology for more information.

CHAPTER 5: WHY DO WE LISTEN TO THE PUBLIC?

Why do we listen to the Public?

In the last few chapters, we have looked at why the public's opinion can be flawed, so the question is why would the government or officials listen to the public when it's often wrong?

The reason we need to listen to the public is that the Halliday report (Home Office 2000) recognised that public opinion is important in sentencing as the public need to have confidence in the Criminal Justice System in an effort to prevent vigilante justice and the public upholds the law.

It's important to know that public opinion is important but it isn't essential, and sentences shouldn't be decided on whether or not the public will agree with you.

Another rather interesting way to think about this need to listen is that the police and the public have a reciprocal relationship. As a result, the police give the public protection and investigates their crimes in exchange for public cooperation, and vice versa.

Therefore, it's important to listen to the public in order to keep this relationship strong.

Another example would be the public are consumers of the service that the police offers them- so to keep the public continuing to consume these services.

They must be listened to.

In fact, it's no different to a massive company like Apple not listening to their customers and seeing a drop in sales.

Political consequences of public opinion:

There are many important consequences of ignoring public opinion.

Like, 'Confrontation politics' this is when the public confronts the government about its policies.

Such as the 1991 poll tax.

This is when the UK Government drafted the tax bill in 3 months and when it was given to the public for public consultation. It was heavily rejected, but the government ignored these rejections.

Resulting in the many problems for the government. Including the worst riots since world war 2 as well as it was a suggested reason to why the UK Prime Minister Margret Thatcher was forced to resign.

Is listening to the public justified?

Whilst some people believe that politicians should not listen to the non or ill-informed public because of their ignorance and the public doesn't pay attention.

When it comes to certain areas like crime. The public is very concerned and pays closer attention to politicians.

This attention to political actions feeds into processes. Like, voting and this is where party support comes from.

However, if a policy was always based on opinion then they would have other problems. Due to public opinion is likely to erratically change so governments would be indecisive.

Then if public opinion is ignored officials risk being voted out.

Public opinion is a vital component of the Criminal Justice System but the public need to develop an opinion based on facts. (Green, 1996)

As mentioned in previous chapters, the problem with opinion polls is that they are often 'top of the head', as well as evidence, suggests that this attitude comes from a lack of evidence and understanding of how the system operates and treats offender.

Common misconceptions:

Some of these misconceptions that the public has about the Criminal Justice System including, the belief that crime is rising, an overestimation in the rates of violent crimes, a lack of knowledge regarding sentencing and an underestimation of the use of prison for serious offenders.

But where does this knowledge come from?

Building upon previously mentioned knowledge sources, knowledge of the Criminal Justice System comes from:

- Jury duty
- Witnesses
- Secondary victimisation
- Direct or indirect experience.

Listening to public opinion:

Building upon the last section, we'll now be looking at the reasons and benefits of listening to public opinion.

Firstly, listening to the public allows the

police and other governmental bodies to create boundaries with the public. Therefore, the public can support and accept the policies.

An example of this would be the stop and search power that the police have since this policing power is a near-perfect balance between the public's right to walk and travel without fear of being unnecessarily searched by the police and the police's ability to search suspicious vehicles or people in the name of public protection.

Another reason to listen to the public and form a two-way dialogue is by listening to the public you can learn what the public is misinformed or underinformed about.

Thus, the police can inform the public about an action or decision.

For example: why they didn't try an 18-year-old as an adult.

However, as this book has mentioned before, this misinformation or people being underinformed is mainly because of the media. As their reports are generally bias and very selective.

Finally, this misinformation or under-information results in a very negative result. For instance, there are or can be low levels of public opinion in the Criminal Justice System.

Meaning that the public are less likely to like, trust or want to help the Criminal Justice System and I hope that this book will help you to appreciate the Justice system more. As if these low levels continue then perhaps one day our justice system may be ineffective as no one wants to help them.

An example of this misinformed business is that contrast to popular belief is the Criminal Justice System is more open to change than people think.

The last reason why listening to the public is needed is because when the public supports your scheme then this support enhances its effect.

PART TWO: COURTS AND THE LEGAL SYSTEM

CHAPTER 6: COURTS AND THE LEGAL SYSTEM

I absolutely love courts.

I love what they represent and their function.

Yet most of all I love the psychology behind them and that's why we'll be investigating them in these next few chapters.

Note: Whilst, we will be focusing on the UK legal system I will still be making references to the European legal system as well as the American legal system.

As an introduction to this topic, we'll

first be looking at the two types of legal systems.

Adversarial system:

This is the legal system that the United Kingdom and the United States tend to use and in this system, the trial is a contest between the prosecution and defence were they call witnesses, cross-examine and present evidence to try to win over the other.

Furthermore, the questioning is governed by strict rules where the judge acts as the umpire with the presumption being innocent until proven guilty.

It's the barrister's job to present a compelling argument for the offender's guilty.

Whilst, it's the defence's job to challenge the soundness of the case. However, interestingly; and I was surprised when I learned this fact, but the defence doesn't have to prove their client's innocence.

Additionally, when it comes to the burden of proof in the Adversarial system when it comes to criminal cases were a law or regulation has been broken. The burden of proof is beyond reasonable doubt.

Whereas in civil cases where a moral wrong has been committed it's all about the balance of probability.

An example for the criminal case would be X killed someone in a road accident; so, a law has been broken. In order to meet the burden of proof and charge X with the crime. The judge or jury would have to be certain beyond reasonable doubt that X did kill this person.

Whereas, for a civil case were a member

of the family was rear-ended in their car. In order to charge the person driving the car who rear-ended them. The judge would have to balance the probability of whose fault it was and it would have to be more probable in order to charge them with the crime.

Lastly, when the UK legal system and the US system was compared a number of differences were found. For example, the UK system improved memory of evidence presented and juror's confidence in their verdict as well as the influence of judges non-verbal cues.

On the other hand, the two systems failed to demonstrate how the two different systems affect the trial outcome.

The Inquisitorial system:

Before, we dive into what the inquisitorial system is.

I have to say that I love this system but not for the reason that you think.

Personally, I am nearly obsessed with the Inquisition.

I love the word Inquisition.

Mainly because I love the sci-fi fantasy universe of Warhammer 40,000 and they have an Inquisition and their Inquisitors are amazing.

Therefore, whenever I come across something to do with the Inquisition or something related. I quickly become interested.

Anyway, now that the fanboy stuff is over. Let's learn about the Inquisitorial Legal System.

What is the Inquisitorial system?

This is the legal system that is dominant in mainland Europe and in this legal system judges play a greater role where they act as investigating magistrates. Where they decide which witnesses to call and they direct police efforts.

In other words, the line between the police and the court is blurred because as mentioned in the Adversarial explanation the police are one separate entity then the judge and prosecution serve is another entity.

However, for the Inquisitorial system, this isn't the case.

As a result, judges have a more active role, lawyers take more of a secondary role. Resulting in less procedural rules.

The adversarial British system could be a response to the historical shortcoming of the Inquisitorial system.

The inquisitorial 'jury' is a made up of a judge and laypeople.

Scotland's version of the Inquisitorial System:

Oddly enough Scotland is the only place in the UK that has a very interesting hybridised model of this system called: Procurator Fiscals. (PF)

These Procurators are involved in all sudden and suspicious deaths as well as they undertake preliminary investigations, precognition from witnesses and they prosecute the crimes for the Criminal Justice System, allowing them to direct the police investigations.

Precognition in Scottish law is when you take statements from witnesses after the offender has been charged but before the trial begins.

Extra information:

Here are two extra-legal concepts for you to understand that is key in many legal matters.

Mens Rea- the state of mind that recognises the act was criminal.

Actus Reus- the actual committing of the criminal act.

In the UK, when it comes to a corner's inquest or case involving the care of children. These matters are closer to the inquisitorial system than the adversarial system.

Sevier (2014) compared the two systems and it turns out that in terms of the 'truth-justice trade-off' the adversary system gets closer to delivering to justice than truth and the Inquisitorial system is better at finding the truth.

Government and Courts:

Parliament and the courts try to strike a balance between the right of citizens and the police's powers.

Although, this co-existence does depend on the political mood at the time.

For example, if the public is restless and demanding the government to do more to tackle crime then this can cause the government to be very demanding of the Courts. Hence, making co-existence difficult.

As recently, politicians have been trying to extend police powers. By trying to restrict bail rights and reduce the right to silence.

Consequences:

The double effect (Foot, 1967) is when the perceived consequences and the intended consequences are different.

For example, Keegan (2011) argues that whilst information from torture is likely to be unreliable. It has the unintended effect of likely radicalising the victim's associates.

When do courts require Forensic Psychologists?

Forensic psychologists can be used in the prosecution process because they can assess whether or not a person is fit to plead.

Fitness to plead is fundamental in British Law (Rogers et al, 2008)

Rogers and his colleagues outline key criteria for assessing fitness to plead.

- Ability to pled
- Ability to understand the evidence against them.

- Ability to understand court proceeding
- Ability to instruct a lawyer
- Knowing that a juror can be challenged

CHAPTER 7: TYPES OF COURTS AND THE YOUTH JUSTICE SYSTEM

In England and Wales, all cases whether they are civil; like an injury; or a criminal case; like murder; start in the Magistrates court then if the case is more serious then the Magistrates will pass the case onto the Crown Court.

Magistrates courts:

In the Magistrates Court, cases are heard by 2-3 lay Magistrates or 1 district judge, as well as there are three types of offences that are heard.

The first type of offence is called a

summary offence. These are less serious offences. For example public nudity.

The second type is called an Indictable offence. These are more serious offences that must first be subjected to a hearing before being passed onto the Crown Court.

Finally, there are either way offences. These are offences that can be dealt with by the Magistrates Court or Crown Court. Generally, depending on the seriousness. For instance: theft, assault and burglary.

Crow Courts:

Moving onto Crown Courts, there are three classes of offences that are heard.

- Class 1 offences- these are the most serious offences and are normally heard by a high court judge. For example terrorism.

- Class 2 offences- these offences are still serious not as serious as the Class 1 offences. Like rape.
- Class 3 offences- these include all other offences and are heard by a Circuit Judge or a Recorder.

In 2017, there were over 114, 340 cases heard in the Crown Courts and of these cases only 9,816 cases were appeals.

In addition, 67% of offenders entered the court pleading guilty and on average it took 25 weeks for the case to be heard and finished.

Youth Justice System:

In the UK, the Youth Justice System is for 10-17-year-old children as the UK has an age of criminal responsibility of 10 years old.

The Youth Justice System differs from the other types of courts in several ways.

For example, The Youth system is less formal than the adult system and the cases are heard by 3 Magistrates or a single District Judge.

Subsequently, the biggest difference between the Youth Justice System and the adult system must be that the public isn't allowed into the courtroom without permission, as well as a guardian must be present.

Finally, instead of being subjected to prison time youth offenders can be given a Youth Rehabilitation Order. In essences, this is a court order stating that a youth offender must do one or more of 18 requirements.

Some of these requirements include:

- Custodial curfew
- Have to be Supervised
- Unpaid work

- Go for drug treatment
- Meet an education requirement

Lastly, youth offenders can be given a custodial sentence. These sentences are served in a secure childhood's home, a secure training centre or youth offence institute.

Youth Offender Statistics:

As of August 2019, the following statistics give a breakdown of youth offenders from January 2019 to August 2019.

- 416 of the Youth Offenders were white.
- 431 of the Youth Offenders were from a black, Asian or minority background.
- 828 of the offenders were male
- 30 of the offenders were female.

CHAPTER 8: THE COURT ROOM, WITNESSES AND LAWYERS

Now that we've looked at the legal foundations of the English system. We can start to look at the workings of the courtroom.

Firstly, despite what television would have us believe. In the United Kingdom lawyers are confined and not free to walk around the courtroom when presenting their case.

Opening Statements:

The opening statement like all parts of the court procedure is very important as the opening statement outlines the facts of the case.

Basically, the opening statement is an introduction.

Moreover, Mauct and McCrimson (1993) found several vital factors that increase the quality of an opening statement.

- You need to maintain eye contact with the jury.
- The opening statement needs to be 10 minutes or less.
- Don't have notes or you will be seen as incompetent.
- Don't include your opinion
- You need to personalise it.

Another feature that you might want to include in your opening statement is you might want to acknowledge weaknesses in the case (Maut, 2002)

For example: "Yes X was seen with a knife in their hands, but nobody saw him actually kill her"

Although, one of the most important things to remember is NOT to make the jury feel manipulated.

Otherwise, they will turn against you.

Evidence:

In court cases, the evidence is always suspect or questioned because everything is open to interpretation and a great lawyer can spin anything into something else.

For example:

- Just because someone's fingerprints are on the victim doesn't mean that they killed them. The fingerprints could have got on the victim when they danced together at the night club earlier in the evening.

- Whilst, the murder weapon was found in her garden it doesn't make her a killer as surely someone could have framed her. Especially, as there's an alleyway next to her garden so it wouldn't be hard to throw something over the fence. I mean just look how low the fences are.

Overall, I hope that those two quick fictional examples showed you how evidence is always suspicious and open to interpretation.

This suspicion is even more important as we convict based on 'beyond reasonable doubt' so if there is any reasonable doubt then the prosecution's case can fail.

Structural constraints within the courtroom:

Within the courtroom, there are many constraints that inhibit the work of both the prosecution and the defence team-yet these constraints are generally for the betterment of the accused.

Two examples of these constraints include:

- Restrictions on the use of information about previous offences.
- The prosecution goes first.

Presentation and Order of Case

In court cases, the way you present a case WILL make or break your case, because if you are unprofessional and clumsy then the jury will most probably be in favour for the other side.

Showing the importance of order and presentation in more detail is when Bennett and Feldrea (1981) found a few important ways that you need to think about a case in order to present it well.

Firstly, you need to see the case as a story as you are telling the jury or judge the events of what happened. Therefore, the number of events needs to flow as a good story does and it is the structural properties of the 'story' that far outweigh other factors in the perception of a case.

In other words, you could have the best evidence that proves that he or she is guilty. Yet if your story is bad then you will still fail.

Equally, if you have weak evidence but a thrilling and logical story then your side could still win.

Additionally, the researchers found the primacy and recency effect are important in courts as well.

These effects state that the first arguments made tend to be more persuasive but for a long trial the arguments at the end are the most important.

Nonetheless, the middle of the arguments isn't important for neither the prosecution nor defence. (Barlett and Memon, 1995)

Lawyers:

In their quest for *truth and Justice*, lawyers must use a wide range of strategies to persuade the Judge and Jury that their client is innocent or that the accused is guilty.

Strategies with some examples include:

- Vivid language- like: he smashed her skull into the toilet seat instead of he knocked her skull.
- Repetition
- Loaded question- why did you kill your wife?
- Subtle shifts in wording
- Manipulate the creditability of a witness- like: you graduated from the University of X, didn't you doctor. Wasn't that the university that falsified all their student's coursework to give them better marks?
- Powerful speech style
- Making witnesses appear incompetent

Source: Bennet and Feldman (1981)

Furthermore, lawyers can construct narratives using:

- Definitional tactics

- Informational tactics
- Validation tactics

Here's a quick look at two very interesting pieces of extra information:

- Litigation is a form of combat and good lawyers excel at combat. (Dabbs, Alford and Fielden, 1998)
- Dabs et al (1998) found that trials lawyers have higher levels of testosterone than non-trial lawyers regardless of gender.

Witness Conduct and Job of the Counsel:

With witnesses being a vital pillar of the Criminal Justice System, it is important that there are rules in place to support the witness and the efforts of the court in finding the *truth or Justice*.

One example is that the council must present witnesses consistent with the story order.

This helps with the flow of the story for both sides of the case and it helps not to confuse the jurors.

Another duty that the Counsel has includes helping the witness to relive the event so the counsel can glean all information from them.

Overall, the expert witness section of the trial is merely a simple logical examination of the witness and get their professional opinion on the crime.

Additionally, it is important for the Council to vary the speed of their questioning as appropriate so they can effectively fast forward to the relevant pieces of information, use open questioning and to ask the witness to clarify something that needs it.

As discovered by Evans (1995) during

Cross-examination the council must:

- Be kind to the other side
- Have purpose in question
- Ask in the spirit of enquiry, not hostility
- Control witness- ask short questions and best questions first (primacy, recency effects)

Eyewitness testimony:

This topic I find amazing because eyewitness testimonies are core to the Criminal Justice System.

However, these testimonies are often wrong due to several factors including facial distinctiveness. This is where highly attractive or unattractive people are easier to recognize (Carlson, 2011)

Note: for more information about the psychology behind these effects and the flaws in the human memory, please check out Cognitive Psychology by Connor Whiteley.

In addition, attractive people are treated better in the Criminal Justice System.

- Change blindness- this is when suspects change their appearance which makes identification less accurate.

Although, my Forensic Psychology Lecturer did say that if you focus on the shoes of a suspect or attacker then you can identify them better.

This is because suspects rarely change their shoes.

- Weapon focus (Slabloy, 1992)- were you focus on the weapon the attacker is holding instead of the attacker themselves.
- Target salience- if there's a lot of people around like in a busy city

street then it's harder to identify a perpetrator.

- Crime seriousness- the more serious the crime the more accurate the memories are due to higher levels of arousal. Meaning you have the better acquisition of the information.

In other words, flashbulb memories.

Please see Cognitive Psychology for more information.

Some additional factors include:

- Stereotypes
- Age
- Post-event information
- Intoxication
- false memories

Some other problems with eyewitnesses include:

- They over-estimate the duration of events.
- Unconscious transference- they sometimes identify a culprit as a person from another context.
- They use their common sense despite common sense being wrong (Deffenbacher and Loftus, 1982)

Expert witness:

In the Criminal Justice System, there's a wide range of expert witnesses that can be called to the stand. Including:

- Medical doctors
- Psychologists
- Police Officers

As a result of their expertise in a particular field, expert witnesses are treated very differently to *normal* witnesses as expert witnesses are allowed to express their own opinion.

Although, they aren't allowed to offer evidence outside the terms of their expertise.

For example, a medical doctor couldn't give evidence on psychological matters because psychology is outside their expertise.

Closing arguments:

After looking at the trial and how a trial works, we arrive at the last part of the trial. Which are the closing arguments.

In short, you should chronologically run through to reinforce the story (Rieke and Stutmay, 1990) This is best for counsel (Spiecker, 1998) and you could use exploratory approaches to compare opposing views. This is best for defence. (Spiecker, 1998)

Parole boards:

On the next stage of the criminal journey after prison time is the parole broad deciding whether to put the offender on parole.

The parole broad carries out risk assessments and manages:

- Early releases of prisoners serving a fixed sentence of at least 4 years.
- Release of prisoners serving life or indeterminate sentences of imprisonment for public protection.
- Recommendation of suitability for transfer to open prisons.

The primary aim of the broad is public protection, but parole can be counted as part of the rehabilitation process as well

Typically, the broad receives a file that includes a judge's remarks, the offender's past convictions, and reports from probation and prison staff. Subsequently, the parole broad examine statistic and practical features in a panel before deciding to take the decision to a full oral hearing or not.

There's a victim impact statement and the number of courses taken by the offender is considered as well.

In the hearing, there are usually 3-panel members and sometimes a psychologist or psychiatrist.

The issues at stake are whether the offender is a risk or not.

CHAPTER 9: JURIES AND PROBLEM WITH JURIES

Judicial decision:

Typically, a jury is made up of 12 lays people.

Before 1967, the jury needed to agree on the verdict but ever since 1967 a majority is accepted.

In total in England and Wales, only 2% of all criminal cases are put in front of a jury.

Problems with juries:

There are a lot of problems within the Criminal Justice System and juries is one of the problems for a few reasons.

What is a peer?

This is a problem because the whole idea of a jury is to be tried by your peers, but how do you define a peer?

For instance, I am an 18-year psychology student studying at university who is an independent author as well.

Therefore, could I be considered a peer to a 50-year-old who never went to university?

Equally, would a 60-year-old Doctor of Medicine be considered a peer when compared to me?

Juror Competence:

Unlike the competence of witnesses, a juror's competence doesn't need to be established so a juror could have no understanding of right, wrong, up or down and it doesn't matter.

Therefore, if there are incompetent jurors on the jury then surely this harms the judicial process as these incompetent people could influence the verdict. Possibly leading to a miscarriage of justice.

Lack of attendance:

However, another problem with juries is a lack of attendance because in 2018 there were 598,605 jurors summoned and only 83,712 turned up.

Presenting us with a problem because if jurors don't turn up then they can't hear the cases and deliver Justice.

Although, you can say no if it's a distressing case or if you have a holiday booked. If so, you can defer but you still must serve on a jury.

Generally, you can very rarely say no to a jury summons.

Does random selection guarantee a fair trial?

Whilst this section does skew towards the more dramatic USA legal system, this example still applies to the UK system.

Trials by their very nature are designed to be fair so the *truth or justice* can be carried out, but there's no guarantee that random selection will give you a representative jury.

As a result, this is very difficult as there are many different minority and majorities to account for in the jury selection.

Finally, even if you do manage to get a representative jury then this doesn't make it impartial, because everyone will bring certain bias with them, as well as gender differences.

For instance, a British-African person who's serving on a jury against a racist attacker could potentially be more likely to convict or be biased.

Another example is that a Juror that is pro-death penalty is more likely to convict.

Nonetheless, some real-life studies show there is no relationship between the outcome and the composition of the jury.

Possibly meaning that the jury makes up isn't important after all.

Additional problems:

Below are some additional issues with juries:

- Despite a judge's instruction to disregard or ignore the jury still remembers the information and is influenced by it.
- Pre-trial publicity influences a jury's decision and as previously mentioned the media is bias.
- Even when a confession has been retracted from evidence and the jury learn of it. They are heavily influenced by this information.
- If the accused is attractive, then the jury is less likely to convict.
- Jurors have an overreliance on eyewitnesses despite research that states that when asked to make a cross-cultural ID. It's easier and we're more likely to make a correct identification if that person is from the same ethnic group as us. Like: white people are better at Identifying other white people.

Case studies:

Servance et al (1982) found that jurors have problems with fine legal definitions.

Halte et al (1983)- jurors have poor recall of trial information. The USA have voire dire process to combat bias.

Deliberations:

It is generally believed that jurors have already decided before deliberations have started and it's a sad truth that in the deliberations instead of focusing on the accuracy of the decision; that can change someone's life; jurors instead focus on reaching a consensus.

In addition, as only a majority is needed some jurors don't even take part in the discussions and Zeisel (1971) found the larger the jury. The greater the chance of a hung jury.

Possible alternatives:

We're looked at the problems that juries represent for the Criminal Justice System, but are there any alternatives?

One alternative would be to have a single or panel of judges deciding on the verdict.

Whilst, another alternative would be to have a mixture of laypeople and judges.

Nevertheless, both alternatives have similar problems as judges tend to dominate discussions and ultimately decide on the faith of the accused, as well as a judge's experience tends to lead to higher conviction rates.

In other words, increasing the chances of an innocent person going to prison.

Hope for Juries:

On the other hand, Mathews et al (2000) found that serving on a jury has a lot of benefits for developing knowledge of the Criminal Justice System.

As a result, the researchers found after jury duty, jurors reported an increased understanding of the Criminal Justice System and they were more positive regarding the Justice System, as well as they were more positive of the judge's competence.

Meaning that juries despite their problems can be very useful and they hopefully will always remain a central pillar of Justice System.

Connor Whiteley

PART THREE: SEX OFFENDING

CHAPTER 10: SEXUAL OFFENDING

Sexual offending is a horrific crime- so what drives someone to commit this dreadful act and what's the psychology behind it?

That will be the focus of this chapter.

Firstly, laws can be problematic for research purposes. For example: if we wanted to research people who committed statutory rape then laws are very problematic as the age of consent is different between countries. Meaning that this person may be considered a criminal in one country but legal in another country.

To emphasise the scope of this terrible crime is that according to MacDonald (2000) 1 in 5 women will experience rape or attempted rape.

Junk Statistics:

In the world, there are a lot of 'junk statistics from advocacy groups' (Pinker, 2011) such as 1 in 4 university students have been raped.

This refers to stats that exaggerate the prevalence and cherry-picking stats for personal and political gain. This can happen in research as well as for funding purposes.

The problem with these statistics is that the definitions they used were way too broad. Such as regretful sex was classed as rape.

This is rarely the case in reality because I know people who have had regretful sex and it has been very consensual.

General statistics for sexual offences:

In the US, the annual rates of rape have decreased over the years by 80% since 1973 compared to only a 57% reduction in homicide. (Pinker, 2011)

In addition, the latest UK estimates are that 430,000 to 517,000 sexual offences are committed each year.

Overall, showing that whilst sexual offending is still a problem. We can come a long way.

Finally, a meta-analysis has stated that global rates of child sexual abuse are 4-19% boys and 11%-22% girls. (Stolenborogh et al, 2014)

Meaning that 4%-19% of the world's

global boy population is sexually abused.

What type of person molests children?

In the next few sections, we'll be looking at sexual offending against children but first, we need to bust some myths.

Wortley (2009) examined misconceptions and Smallbone and Worthley (2006;2004) found that for the stranger danger myth that when it came to sexual offending against children. 56.4% of sexual offenders lived with the victims, 36.9% knew the child and only 6.5% of the sexual offenders were strangers. Thus, showing how the stranger danger myth isn't true and that children are more likely to become victims of sexual abuse from people they know or live with.

Subsequently, for the 'paedophiles rings'

myth- the researchers found that only 8% of all sexual offenders talked to other offenders and only 4% of sexual offenders were a part of a ring.

Overall, this shows how the actions of a very small minority can be powerful enough to create myths about sex offenders and trick society into becoming overly fearful.

'most individuals who commit sexual offences against a child are gay'

I will jump in straight at the start of this section and state this is false because research has shown that when the stated orientations of a male sex offender are analysed 76% of male sex offenders are heterosexual, 13% of male sex offenders are interested in both male and females and only 8% of all sex offenders are homosexual.

Consequently, it's unlikely to be raped by a homosexual as the research demonstrates that the majority of sex offenders are heterosexual so prefer females.

On the other hand, male on male rapists can more victims on average.

Are all abusers paedophilic?

Paedophiles are very commonly used in the media and to describe the act the sexually offending against children, but it's often used incorrectly. As I'll show you in this next section.

Firstly, Paedophiles refer to the asexual interest in children, so Paedophiles are attracted to children, but they don't want to have sex with them necessarily.

In fact, it's the child molesters that have a sexual interest in children.

Another difference between child molesters and Paedophiles is that paedophilia involves puberty or prepuberty children. Whereas child molesters can be sexually attracted to other age groups of children. For example, Hebephilia which is children around the age of puberty and Ephebophilia which the age of adolescent.

Overall, you can be a paedophile, but you don't have to be an offender.

In addition, 40%-50% of offenders who commit contact offences are paedophiles. (Seto, 2008) This includes people who are interested in children.

Virtuous paedophiles:

These next two sections are an interesting read and definitely food for thought so please keep reading and I'll add my opinion at the end.

Virtuous paedophiles is a website and a group of paedophiles that didn't want to the offender and created a supportive network. Because other forums at the time were focused on getting paedophiles decriminalised and how to access child pornography.

People on the forum displayed both practical methods. Like: only doing shopping during school time and other methods. Like: consequential thinking-thinking about the consequences of the sexual urge on self, child and more. In order to prevent themselves from sexually offending.

Dunkelfeld project, Germany.

The project's aim was to create acceptance in the research and clinical community that they knew nothing about paedophiles that were never caught and they got money to interact as well as study people that were inaccessible before such as paedophiles who don't offend.

Personally, I think that it's good that there's a place that these people can go to stop themselves acting offending and destroying a child's life, as well as there's research into these inaccessible areas.

However, we need to make sure that this website doesn't offer an excuse to allow people to see their paedophiles as uncontrollable or predetermined. As this 'uncontrollable' mindset could be very dangerous for society and it would put a lot of doubt into treatment programmes.

As for the German project, is it worth spending tons of money on low risk compared to high-risk offenders?

Personally, I don't think it is because if these people don't offend then… you could potentially say that they aren't a threat to society so I strongly believe that it's more important to put the money into the people who offend and are threats to society.

Most importantly, I believe that it's important to put money into treatment so these sex offenders can be treated and returned to society so these people can live good lives.

How do we measure sexual interest?

I will fully confess when we had the lecture on this topic, the lecturer told us about this very interesting device that the researchers used to use to investigate someone's sexual interest.

This technique was a piece of equipment that you attached to the man's penis and showed him images of men, women, children with an audio clip as well, also there was a bondage clip that had an audio track with the sound of breaking bones.

The point of this was to see how much blood rushed to the penis because of the man's sexual arousal.

Hearing that device was an odd piece of the lecture.

Though, there are problems with these traditional techniques. For example, they don't help to build rapport or trust and trust is a very important ineffective treatment. Meaning that this is likely to be harmful to successful treatment.

In addition, these techniques have questionable reliability and validity. In other words, it's questionable if they actually test sexual interest, as well as these techniques, are useless if a sex offender has erectile dysfunction.

Therefore, less direct methods are now being developed. Such as: looking at reaction time to stimuli- as people get distracted by stimuli, they find sexually appealing. (O'Ciardla and Gromley, 2012)

On a quick departing note, child molestation can offend against children without paedophiles interest, as well as incest tends to have less evidence of paedophiles with lower re-offending rates.

Child pornography:

Here's another extremely questionable area of life because of child pornography... there's no easy way to discuss this topic. Especially, considering what some children have to go through.

There has been a lot of research into child pornography but the main problem with this research is that it was done pre-internet. When the typical sex offender had to go out and meet people to exchange child pornography.

This presents a problem for research because it gives it a temporal validity issue; where the progression of time affects the results; as you could find that the results from this early research is pointless in today's interconnected internet world. As these days sex offenders could 'easily' find child pornography online.

Moreover, people that are apprehended with child pornography show greater paedophilic arousal than contact offenders. (Seto et al, 2006) but this is not a direct correlation.

The reason why this isn't a direct correlation is that when the media says something like 'X was found with 5,000 hours of child pornography on their laptop' the media fails to mention what other collections of other taboo or non-illegal porn. They have as sometimes it can be far, far much more than the child pornography on their laptop.

Additional information on treatment:

As a result of these findings, different treatment is needed for sex offenders as 1 in 8 people record, they have committed a contact offence (official record) and 50% self-reported contact offence.

Showing that there is a difference between the official records and the reality of the world, but you must remember that self-reported data isn't always reliable.

Female predators:

I know that the media and people in general always think sex offenders to be male and they are right to some extent as males are the majority of the sex offender population.

However, it must be remembered that females can and do still commit sexual offences against men, women and children.

Sadly, the literature on female sexual offending is limited and certain areas are a lot more researched than others. Meaning that this section I can't explore the topic as much as I would like to.

Firstly, here are some general statistics for female sexual offending 4% of all sexual offences are caused by females but only 1% of the prison population is female.

Yet the very interesting part is that there's a mismatch between the number of females who commit offences and are convicted. As 1 in 20 females commit sexual offences but only one in a hundred are convicted.

This I find extremely interesting because this could be for several reasons. Such as people would be in disbelieve that a woman could commit an offence or the women were attractive and can increase the likelihood of not getting convicted or another of the many reasons.

It's good to think about though.

Moving into another reason for female sexual offending is that many but not all women co-offend with a male.

Equally, it's important to note that women can freely to co-offend with a male or they can be coerced into co-offending.

Finally, another reason why people may be less willing to convict a woman is that they could underestimate females as social and cultural constructs could state women abusers as less harmful and if a victim is abused by a woman then they could less empowered to report it.

Types of rapists:

In the world, there are apparently five types of rapists. I say apparently because I'm still open to the idea that there could be more types but the five types of rapists are:

- Anger and excitation or sadistic
- Anger retaliation
- Power assurance
- Power dominance
- Opportunity

According to Penatky and Knight

(1991), opportunistic rapists can be divided into high and low social compliance and sadistic can be divided into muted and overt.

In other words, some rapists are more discreet than others.

Types of people who rape:

There are many types of rape that exist in this world including:

- Marital rape- where you rape the person you're married to.
- Acquaintance rape- you rape an acquaintance or friend.
- Date rape- you rape the person you're on a date with.
- Multiple perpetrator rape- a contrast to popular belief about 25% of all rapes are this kind where you're raped by multiple people.

These multiple rapists can include:

- North American fraternities
- Gangs
- Rape in war
- Prison rape- US DOJ estimates 216,000 victims of sexual assault in US prisons and roughly 1 in 10 in US prisons population are victims.

CHAPTER 11: THEORIES OF SEXUAL OFFENDING

An integrated theory of sexual assault (Ward and Beech, 2006;2017)

This theory looks at a lot of different functions or features that can make up sexual offending behaviour.

Here are some of the areas covered and we'll be exploring them in more depth later:

- Neuropsychological functioning
- Clinical symptoms and state functioning
- Sexual offending
- Maintenance escalation

- Ecological niche and brain development (genetics and evolutionary)

According to this theory, there's a link between genetics and sexual offending.

As paedophiles tend to be:

- 10 to 15 IQ points lower than the average person.
- 2.5cm shorter on average
- Huge differences in white matter. (brain glue) (This was a shock to researchers as nothing of interest ever happens in the white matter)
- The brain is hard (crossed) wired to activate neuropathways towards attraction and parental nurture.

The last point means that when the parental pathways in the brain get attracted then this attracts the attraction part of the brain as well. Meaning that the person themselves might be trying to act parentally but due to how their brain is wired they are feeling sexual attraction as well.

Of course, this is no excuse as there are other factors at work here.

Biology:

The latest research suggests pre-natal influences so there are influences before birth that can give rise to sexual offending, but I strongly believe and the research supports this relationship as not a smoking smoke in terms of causation.

Basically, these prenatal influences don't cause sexual offending outright.

Not smoking gun relationships in terms of causation.

Ecological niche:

This ecological niche refers to the environment and the social factors of a person.

Some social actors that can cause sexual offending include the offender's own history of abuse (Glaner et al, 2001), as well as 35% of all male abusers, have been victims themselves.

Group processes:

Another cause of sexual offending behaviour is group processes as these group process can lead to multiple preparator rape as well as rape cases in war.

For more information on group process, please check out my Sociocultural Psychology book.

Neuropsychological functioning:

For sexual offending, this is very compelling because it turns out sexual offenders have a lot of neuropsychological/ cognitive differences in their brains.

For example, as previously discussed there is a massive difference in the setup of certain psychological functions, and sexual offenders have different motivation and they perceive emotion differently to some extent.

In addition, sexual offenders have different world perceptions and memories. They basically have a cognitive distortion where their thinking style is distorted meaning that in essence in their mind they can justify their actions.

Moreover, sex offenders can have an

anti-social personality and they have a regulatory problem where they need sex to regulate their daily life.

Overall, this section is a little vague in the theory and I've tried to flesh these factors out the best I can.

Clinical symptoms include:

The last section of this theory is clinical symptoms; symptoms of a mental disorder in the simplest terms. For example, sex offenders have emotional problems regarding their behaviour, and they have social difficulty. This gives them the need for intimacy.

Additionally, sexual offenders have deviant arousal so they get their sexual arousal in non-typical ways.

Lastly, sex offenders have something called supportive cognitive yet this particularly vague in the theory.

However, it's meant to be something like the sex offender's beliefs makeup excuses for the offender's behaviour.

Youth sex offenders:

In our penultimate section, it's important to remember those sex offenders aren't exclusively dirty old men because as previously showed females can commit sexual offences. Yet youths or young people can as well.

Typically, the factors that cause a young person to sexually offence include:

Being from a low socioeconomic background.

Having pathological family structures and interaction styles.

Having fathers that were neglected as children.

Having mothers that were physically

abused as children.

Overall, throughout this chapter, I hope that you have being to see how devasting simple actions to one person can affect tens of people.

For example: by physically abusing the mother, the mother's child could become a sexual offender, leading to victims, then those victims could become offenders. Leading to more victims until the cycle one-day stops but by then hundreds of people's lives would be damaged or destroyed.

Ultimately, meaning one action is not against one person. It's against potentially hundreds of people.

Theories of paedophiles:

When it comes to the theories of paedophiles, the literature is very limited because precondition models; models that focus on cognition; are historically important but very few have its components empirical supported.

Subsequently, you have psychotherapy and clinical model. These model stress the cognitive aspect of the offending cycle. Such as fantasy and cognitive distortion.

Thankfully, these models have more support and it has a degree of validity in terms of describing the abuse process, but it doesn't explain the development of offending behaviour.

PART FOUR: REHABILATION

CHAPTER 12: REHABILATION OF OFFENDERS

In this chapter, we'll be investigating how offenders are rehabilitated for release into the community once more and the main example in this chapter will be sex offenders.

The main reason why I'll be using sex offenders is that they can be rehabilitated in contrast to the societal view that sex offenders should be locked up and abandoned.

History of sex offender treatment:

The effective treatment of sex offenders didn't start until the 1960s because before that time society believed in the Freudian theory that sexual offenders were untreatable using psychodynamic methods.

Resulting in sex offender treatment being considered an extremely low priority, as well as this thinking, created a culture of 'nothing works'

Following this interest in sex offender treatment, in the UK in the 1980s there was a 50% rise in the number of sexual offences receiving a custodial sentence (or in simpler terms receiving a prison sentence). (Fisher and Beech, 1999)

Although, this rise in prison sentences didn't match a reduction in re-offending.

Meaning sending sex offenders to prison didn't stop them from re-offending.

Subsequently, in the 1990s Cognitive Behavioural Therapy (CBT) was used for sex offender treatment. That aims to restructure the offender's thinking processes and active positive behaviours.

For more information on CBT please check out Abnormal Psychology by Connor Whiteley.

We treat offender to:

- Save prisoner's health and dignity
- To reduce long term determinantal problems in society
- To provide a further perception of justice
- Note not every crime deserve to serve punishment
- Research shows rehabilitation works with some types of offenders better than others.

Rehabilitation and Treatment:

When it comes to treatment programmes regardless of crime it's vital to decide and tailor your programme to the type of offender, what the crime was, where the treatment will be happening and when it will be occurring.

Using a non-criminal example, if a government decided to make all school child take the exact same life skills course then the course would certainly fail.

This is because the programme wasn't designed for each age group or type of student (the Who) as 18-year-olds would need different life skills to an 8-year-old.

Equally, the programmes wouldn't have tailored for the different locations (the Where) that the programme would be carried out. As a rich school could potentially teach the programme far better than a poor school. Resulting in an education inequality for the students.

Overall, I hope that you can see how tailoring a programme for offenders is important.

Therapeutic Treatment for Sex Offender:

This type of treatment for a sex offender is based on group work; so the offender can build and improve their social skills; where you have two groups of 8 sex offenders and 2 tutors or therapists.

Within this group work, some techniques that are used to help treat the offenders include:

- Brainstorming and group-decision.
- Groups that focus on the individual, the work of one individual is subject to scrutiny

and evaluation by the rest of the group

- Homework- such as keeping a diary
- Roleplaying
- Smaller groups- help to develop skills, assertiveness and degrees of empathy.
- Videos- helpful for educating offenders.

In addition, the following areas are covered using these methods:

- Describing the offence- seeing how the offender sees their actions so the treatment can show them how what they did was wrong.
- Challenges distorted thinking- sexual offenders; as mentioned previously; have a distorted way of thinking so their actions are

deemed fine according to their thinking.

- Victim's empathy work- the offender can empathise with their victim and hopefully not do it again as they know how it will destroy that person's life.

Fantasy modification:

Personally, when I read this section in one of my psychology textbooks I was equally interested as a future psychologist and horrified because well… it was a bit graphic to read.

Hopefully, my version will be PG-rated and still useful.

Sex offenders like all of us have fantasy and most of us will never act on our fantasy yet sex offender typically do, and it's these fantasies that need modifying as its these fantasies and other factors that drive sex offender to commit the act.

Therefore, these fantasies can be modified on an individual level with the help of a psychologist.

Some techniques that the psychologist can use to modify these fantasies include:

- Aversive therapy- you pair fantasy with a very unpleasant sensation.
- Masturbatory reconditioning- you effectively restructure the offender's thinking patterns so they no longer find the fantasy attractive or to put it more colloquially a 'turn on'
- Saturation- the offender repeatedly masturbates until the fantasy no longer elicits orgasm.

Overall, in treatment, it is important to develop the offender's social skills, assertiveness and anger control before they are released back into society.

Due to developing these skills will help to decrease the likelihood of re-offending.

Cognitive programs are very effective because they get offenders to shift the criminal mindset and they focus on risk factors for criminal re-offending.

These programs involve:

- Interpersonal skill training
- Behavioural technique such as modelling, graduated practice, role-playing
- Cognitive skills training (different ways of thinking)
- Structured induvial counselling for problem-solving training.
- cognitive and behavioural treatment

This type of programmes assumes that

offenders are shaped and influenced by the environment and it completely ignores biological factors.

In addition, the program assumes that they've learned 'bad' or maladaptive behaviour and failed to learn effective cognitive and behavioural skills for proper functioning in society.

In other words, the offenders have developed behaviour that makes it difficult to adapt and function in society.

In cognitive programs, treatment involves:

- problem-solving training
- social skills training
- pro-social modelling

Cognitive behavioural treatment is considered the most effective treatment because it's very similar to Cognitive Behavioural Therapy as used in the treatment of Depression.

To learn more about Cognitive Behavioural Therapy then please check out Abnormal Psychology.

Finally, taking hasher approaches are not very effective. They can help but generally, they are not effective.

CHAPTER 13: PROBLEMS AND CHALLENGES FOR TREATMENT

Unfortunately, there are a lot of challenges that treatment programmes face when delivering treatment, as well as without these problems it is likely that treatment would be better.

The problems include but aren't limited to:

The introduction of new penal policies that favour harsher sentences because as you'll see in the Effects of Imprisonment chapter harsher sentences don't work.

Meaning that offenders are getting

harsher sentences without the treatment. Making them more likely to re-offend.

Another problem for treatment is that the treatment is being delivered by less skilled and less experienced workers. Meaning that offenders can get a lower quality of treatment, so they are less likely to respond to treatment. Making them more likely to re-offend.

Problems with research:

As always nothing is perfect, so why should treatment research be any different?

Meta-analysis is common within research as they allow researchers to find an average of the behaviour or treatment option they are trying to find.

Nevertheless, if an outlier; a study with very different results to the others; is included this can skew the entire results.

Giving them an 'untrue' average.

Additionally, you'll continue to see mentions of research flaws throughout this book.

Failing to complete treatment:

Another problem for treatment is that about 25% of offenders fail to complete treatment. (McMieran and Theodois, 2007)

This has obviously negatives as the offenders don't get the benefit of the full treatment. Making them more likely to re-offend.

Building upon further, Wormith and Oliver (2002) found several reasons why offenders fail to complete their treatment.

Firstly, there are administrative problems where a prisoner gets released earlier than intended or moved to another prison. Resulting in them failing to complete the treatment.

Secondly, the offender gets removed from treatment due to their uncontrollable or disruptive behaviour.

Finally, the offender decides to stop treatment.

Overall, resulting in offenders failing their treatment course.

Why does failing to complete treatment matter?

Besides the facts that I've already spoken about this study demonstrates why treatment matters in a great and possibly scary manger.

Dutton, Bodnarchuk, Kropp and Hart (1997) found the damaging effects that failure to complete treatment can have when they have studied a group of wife beaters in Canada.

Their results broke down in the following ways:

Out of the people didn't that never turned up 9% of these people re-offended.

Out of everyone who the treatment wasn't suitable for 20% of them re-offended.

Out of the dropouts, 11% of them re-offended.

Out of everyone who completed the treatment only 6% of them re-offend.

Knowing that these percentages don't sound a lot- let's translate them into a group of one thousand offenders.

No shows would commit 90 offences.

People that were unsuitable would commit 200 offences.

People who dropped out of treatment would cause 110 offences.

Finally, completers would only commit 60 offences.

Consequently, treatment is associated with fewer offences and many more studies support these findings.

CHAPTER 14: TREATING VIOLENT OFFENDERS

Does anger management work?

In recent years, anger management courses have been called into question because of their lack of effectiveness.

The National Anger Management Package includes the following sessions:

Your first session is an introduction, so you learn about the aims of the course, you keep an anger diary, you learn to understand the bad side of losing your temper and you learn the rules of group conduct.

Following this, in your second session, you focus on changing your behaviour. You learn to recognise the bodily signs of anger and why non-aggressive body language is preferred.

For the third session, it focuses on changing thoughts, so you learn about the relationships between thoughts and behaviour as well as the use of using self-calming statements during anger.

In the fourth session, you focus on controlling your arousal that leads to anger. Therefore, you look at what happens to the body during anger and the ways of dealing with the arousal of anger

Afterwards in your fifth session, you would focus on assertiveness and the differences between passivity, anger and assertiveness.

In your penultimate session, you would focus on handing criticism and insults as these tend to be the main causes of anger. Consequently, you learn the differences between being aware and dealing with group pressure.

Finally, in session 7 and 8 you have an overview of what you're learnt, and you review the programme.

Modern Programmes:

In modern society, we have modernised programmes to take a more in-depth approach to the factors that cause violent behaviour when we treat violent offenders.

In addition, it was Attrill (1999) that are the root of treatment of these modern programmes.

Violence is a learned behaviour that is adopted as a method of coping with difficult life experiences.

This works effectively for the person. Leading to reinforcement in their sense of power and self-efficiency, and patterns of violent and criminal behaviour are intertwined as they both involve supporting ways of thinking.

Consequently, with violence giving people a sense of power and with the patterns showing violence and criminal behaviour are intertwined.

How do we treat these violent offenders?

In the UK, the Aggression Training Programme (ARI) is used. It was developed by (Goldstein, 2004; Goldstein, Glick and Gibbes, 1998)

The programme's basic assumption is that aggression is caused by multiple internal as well as external causes.

Some of these internal causes are general deficits of interpersonal, personal and socio-cognitive skills, frequent implicit impulses of aggression control and moral reasoning deficits

However, given the present state of our knowledge, we cannot make any definitive conclusions about the effectiveness of treatment for violent offending as well as the treatability of high-risk offenders. Like: psychopaths.

Cognitive Behavioural Techniques:

This type of cognitive program works for violent offenders because it gives the offenders a chance to have an insight into why the behaviour in a certain way, as well as it gives them a chance to model new ways of thinking and acting

In these cognitive programs, an offender takes part in activities that:

- recognise the series of events that lead to the outburst or criminal act.
- The resulting emotion
- Techniques for self-assessment
- Practice new behaviours through new play

Research suggest anger management tends to reduce aggression (at least in the short term) but still more research is needed and most violent offenders are resistant to change.

CHAPTER 15: RECOVERY CAPITAL AND MINDSET

Recovery Capital:

Recovery capital is; in essence; the different things that can help people on the road to recovery, and if an offender doesn't have one or more of these capitals than the chance of them re-offending increases.

Granfeild (2009) developed the idea of recovery capital to include:

- Social capital- this is the sense of belonging

This is important for offenders and everyone because if you don't feel like you belong there. You are more likely to rebel from the social norms and commit crimes.

- Physical assets

I personally think about this type of capital as roots and loses because if you have nothing to lose or nothing that keeps you in your local area. Then if you commit crimes and get caught then you haven't got anything tangible to lose.

- Human capital- their health and personal resources.

If an offender has health and has financial, job as well as housing resources then they are less likely to have to commit offences.

- Cultural capital- involves the values, beliefs, and attitudes that allow them to participate in the community.

This links back to the first type of capital as an offender need to feel a part of the community. In order to make them want to protect it.

Mindset for rehabilitation:

Personally, this is very interesting because the mindset is often overlooked when it comes to rehabilitation and I presumed that if you wanted to work in rehabilitation then the sheer desire to work in this area must indicate that you have a good mindset.

Although, the findings below are correct and I do agree with them but they are definitely easy said than done.

Miller and Rollnick (2013) spoke about a mindset and a heart set about rehabilitation:

- Partnership- we work with a person and for them as well as we not to undo them.

An interesting idea and ideally this is true because only through working with another person can we have an impact on them.

Nonetheless, when confronted with a serial rapist with rapes men, women and child as well as they have killed some of their rape victims. Can you honestly tell me that you wouldn't try and undo them and turn them into a new dramatically better person?

- Acceptance- we don't have to approve of their behaviour, but we need to accept that they can change and they have potential.

Again, I do believe in this idea of 'acceptance' but using the same example is it possible to believe that this serial rapist can change?

- Compassion- show compassion to the person we are trying to treat, and we promote their well-being and interest.

Again we need to show compassion to the people we are treating yet how do you show passionate to the serial rapist?

- Evocation- we draw out existing motivation and aim to strengthen this in working alongside the individuals.

Overall, I hope that you can start to understand that you need a positive mindset to work in rehabilitation and see real results, as well as it's difficult to put theory into practice.

CHAPTER 16: REHABILATION THEORIES AND MODELS

Rehabilitation theory: (Ward, Mann and Gannon, 2007)

Rehabilitation is a broad term that refers to the overall aims, values and principles as well as etiological assumptions that guide the treatment of offenders.

More work needs to be done in this area, but a good theory of offender rehabilitation should specify aims of therapy, as well as it needs to justify aims based on assumptions about cause and related factors.

Identify clinical target

It's important to outline treatment based on aetiology (causes) and goals specify the most suitable types of treatment and educate therapist about the best attitude to have.

Risk-Need- Responsivity model:

This model is the dominant model for designing treatment programmes in the UK. (Andrews et al, 2006)

In this model, there are 3 principles that can make rehabilitation effective and they are:

- Risk principles- you match the programme intensity with the offender risk level.
- Need principles- you target criminogenic needs. These are the reasons why the offender committed the crime in the first

place. Like: anger, unemployment and more.

- Responsivity principles- you match the model of intervention and the style with the learning style and ability to the offender. For instance: you would match a visual course with a visual learner.

Research has shown that focusing on all 3 components is better than focusing on only 1 or 2. (Andrews et al, 2006)

Additionally, these programmes are cognitive-based.

Despite large scale use of these types of programmes outcome studies show that it produces poor results, but this could be as a result of poor treatment quality and problems with implementation. (Gorgan and Gendreau, 2006; Young, 2010)

Good Lives Model: Ward and Gannon (2006)

This model is a great model in my opinion because it is very holistic and humane.

Therefore, regarding sexual offending the Good Lives Model (GLM) has 3 components:

- Set of general assumptions/ principles specifying values regarding rehabilitation and the overall aims to strive for.
- Implications of assumptions for understanding and explaining offending and its function
- Treatment implications focusing on goods. Goals, self-regulation strategies and ecological factors.

General principles and assumptions:

The entire model is based on the idea that humans including offenders strive to obtain primary goods.

These are characteristics or states of mind are activities or experiences that increase psychological wellbeing. (Ward, Mann and Gannon, 2007)

Examples of primary goods:

- Life
- Friendship
- Sexual relationships
- Purpose/meaning/spirituality
- Happiness
- Food
- Knowledge (can include skills)

The model mentions secondary goods as well. These are tools or methods that you use to get the primary goods.

The model is based on the concept that sexual offending is a socially unacceptable way to obtain primary goods.

Things to remember:

The model makes no assumption about morality, so it focuses on the pursuit of goods and not necessarily the mortality of outcomes.

Rehabilitation has MANY values. Such as what is best for the offender, what is best for society, the development of knowledge about the problem.

Personal identity is important for the offender should develop a sense of who they are and what it means to have a good life and they should have the opportunity to exercise these factors to have a meaningful.

Psychological well-being and primary

goods need to be accessible, so the offender not to re-offend.

Etiological assumption:

According to the Good Lives Model, sexual offending is caused by a range of factors and sexual abuse occurs as a result of the interaction of various factors.

- Biological- inheritance, brain development
- Ecological niche- contextual situation, social-cultural
- Neuropsychological

Biological and ecological niche factors can impact neuropsychological systems to produce abuse.

- Motivation

- Perception /memory
- Action selection
- Control system
- Abuse

This can lead to various problems that set the contextual for and facilitates abuse:

- Emotional problem
- Empathy deficits
- Social difficulties
- Cognitive distortion
- Deviant sexual arousal

All these factors can combine to create a cycle that scales and/or maintains abuse.

In the Good Lives Model, criminogenic needs are obstacles that block the obtaining of primary goods.

It is the method of acquisition that is the problem, not the goods themselves.

Implications for practice:

Therapy has two goals:

- To promote goods
- Reduce the risk of re-offending

Meaning that we want to provide sexual offenders with skills, values and attitudes and resources for a meaningful life that has primary goods, so this reflects the assumption that the offenders are was seeking goods.

Finally, the model says that therapists should adopt a humanistic attitude toward respect for their capacity to change.

However, this is difficult to do especially when working with the worst offenders.

Risk-Need-Respond versus Good Lives Model:

Critics of the Risk-Need-Responds model prefer the Good Lives Model because the Good Lives Model focuses on the enchantment of the offender and it's a fuller recovery as it uses a strength-based approach and engages dynamic risk factors.

Parting note:

We will have to invest in people no matter what.

But do we invest in the people when they're children or adults?

CHAPTER 17: DOES TREATMENT WORK?

In all honesty, I could easily give you the answer to this vital question but that would make this section very short.

Firstly, it must be said that general society; and this point will be expanded upon in the next chapter; has a very negative attitude when it comes to treatment and people often say:

"Of course, treatment doesn't work"

Therefore, this attitude is important to tackle in the grand scheme of thing because if the public has a lack of faith in treatment then this could lead to political and social consequences.

For instance, politicians don't put

funding into treatment to keep the public happy. Leading to offenders not getting a high quality of treatment as a lower quality is all the prison service can afford. Making the treatment stereotype or attitude true that treatment doesn't work.

Do harsher prison sentences work?

Personally, I MUST stress to you all that longer periods of imprisonment are not associated with a decrease in re-offending.

It all about rehabilitation.

Meaning that our politicians wouldn't be shouted and screamed demanding harsher sentences. They should be focusing on rehabilitation as that's what works to reduce crime.

Further support:

Hood (1996) no relationship between serious crimes and capital punishment has been found across different nations.

Yet these findings did differ by country.

Genedreau, Giggin and Cullen (1999) showed that Canada's longer sentences actually increase re-offending slightly.

Effectiveness of treatment:

Overall, intervention and treatment are largely unsuccessful because for programmes to work, trained staff must be used and appropriate programmes must be used.

On the other hand, Redondo et al (2002) found that Community programmes have the greatest effects.

Additionally, Sex offender programmes had greater effects than programmes for other crimes such as drunk driving. Smith, Goggin & Gendreau (2007)

Duve and Goldman (2009) suggested that there's a more or less consensus that re-offending rates are 5 to 120 points lower with treated groups compared to non-treated groups.

Consequently, this demonstrates that treatment works as offenders that got the treatment was potentially a lot less likely to offend.

However, this study does have two problems. Such as there was no random assignment to groups, and this wasn't a true experiment. Meaning that causality is hard to state outright because as no variables were manipulated. We don't know for certain if it was the treatment that caused the drop in re-offending rates or another factor.

Furthermore, there wasn't a control group; as a group of untreated offenders; so this casts doubt the findings as we don't know if the treatment worked as we cant compare the results to an untreated group of offenders.

Another study that calls the effectiveness of treatment into question is Welsh and Rocque (2014) that discussed that some interventions; such as boost camp; have an adverse effect on offenders.

Personally, I can completely understand this result because I am NOT an offender and I am what society would call a 'good' person, but I do not take orders and I am my own person.

Thus, if I was at a boot camp; why I would be there in the first place is beyond me, and someone was shouting orders at me. Naturally and I believe quite reasonably I would rebel, and my focus would change from trying to learn the benefits of the lesson I was being taught at the Bootcamp to rebelling.

Generally, this is what happens to offenders as well.

Overall treatment findings:

Throughout this section, we have discussed the positives of treatment, the negatives of treatment and everything to do with rehabilitation.

Therefore, in this chapter, I'll tell you that in general, treatment which is defined in many ways tend to show a positive effect.

The mean effect across interventions is small but it includes the interventions that are weak or ineffective.

In other words, some treatment work very well, others work okay and some don't work at all.

The most important thing to remember though is that we have found no magic bullet for treating offenders yet.

PART FIVE: IMPRISONMENT

CHAPTER 18: HISTORY, IMPRISONMENT PRINCIPLES AND PUBLIC OPINON

Before, we explore the effects of imprisonment on offenders. Let's learn about the history of imprisonment.

16th Century:

It all began in the 16th century and in this century, imprisonment was to do with religion as it was a common belief that if someone had committed a crime. Then their body was possessed by evil.

Therefore, imprisonment was meant to punish the body and prison was a place for people that were awaiting trial.

Finally, everyone was imprisoned together, and they had very poor conditions. For instance, malnutrition, maltreatment and disease.

18th century:

This era is a bit more interesting because this is known as the 'Blood code' era where you were punished with the death penalty and jurors decided on the punishment.

Surprisingly though, there were a lot of people that opposed the death penalty for the less serve crimes.

I thought that this was surprising because I thought that back then people would believe in deterring others from crime a lot more- so I thought it reasonable to assume to that they would want to kill others to act as extreme deterrence for others who wanted steal or commit any crime.

Resulting in jurors refused to punish thieves with the death penalty so instead of the death penalty the offenders were sent to British colonies to do hard labour.

During the 18th Century, there was a person called John Howard that insisted on reform and he wanted the following:

- Paid staff to look after prisoners
- Outside inspections to make sure that the offenders were being treated properly.
- A proper diet for the prisoners.
- Men and women should be kept separate.
- Humane living conditions (proper sanitation)

Overall, in the 18th Century, the Humanitarian approach; more on that later; started and the Howard Leverage of Penal Reform was started as well.

Mid-19th Century:

During the Mid-19th Century, imprisonment replaced the death penalty for the most serious offences and more prisons were built.

Additionally, The Prison Act of 1898 was passed. This abolished hard labour and stated that prison labour should be productive and not harmful to the offender's health.

Lastly, the idea of prison should be about reform and reducing re-offending was introduced to the world.

20th century:

In all honesty, the 20th Century was less dramatic with their developments, but one important development was that young people should be kept separate to adults. As adults can influence the younger people with potentially devasting consequences.

Another important development was that the mental needs of the offenders were addressed.

Nevertheless, a very odd and… personally, I find strange development was in 1933, the first open prison was built.

These open prisons are prisons were the offenders can simply walkout during the night and come back at night, yet they were monitored.

I find this idea odd as why didn't the offenders just flee?

Although, Sir Alex Paterson said that "You cannot train a man for freedom under conditions for captivity"

Which makes sense as people do need freedom and not to be caged to be rehabilitated.

What's Important in Punishment?

When it comes to punishment or imprisonment, it important to hold the offender to account so they learn that their actions were wrong as well as not to do them again.

The punishment needs to lead to an 'appropriate' outcome. This can be many forms of punishment. Such as fines, imprisonment, loss of custody of children and more.

Finally, when it comes to punishment, it's important to be confident that serious offenders or serious threats do not pose a threat to public safety. This is the reason why we lock people up in prison as in prison they no longer pose a threat to public safety.

For instance, a rapist cannot rape a member of the public from prison.

The United Nations:

The United Nations have a standard Minimum rule for the treatment of prisoners (1957 / 1997) that must be followed.

Basically, the rules are about complete equality about the treatment of prisoners.

The 19 rules are as followed:

- The prisoners must be registered.
- There must be a separation of categories. Like: men, women and children.
- The prisoners must be provided with good accommodation.

- Prisoners must have the ability to have good personal hygiene. They need to have showers and washing facilities in other words.

- The prisoners must be provided with clothing and bedding.

- They must be provided with food.

- Exercise and sport

- Medical services

- Prisoners should receive discipline and punishment.

- Prisons can be instruments of restraint but they must be ethically used.

- The prisoner must be given information and prisons must listen to complaints by prisoners.

- Prisoners need to have contact with the outside world.

- They should have access to books.

- Prisoners shouldn't be treated differently because of their religion.

- Prisoners should retain their property.

- In addition, they should receive a notification of death, illness, transfer. Either about themselves or a family member.

- And more...

In prisons, the LGBT+ community are very likely to be victimised.

Characteristics of the prison population:

There are many interesting characteristics that are different between the prison and the general population.

For instance: 15% of the general UK population as no qualifications whereas in the prison population 52% of males and 71% of females have no qualifications.

Another example is that in the general

population 23% are homeless yet only 0.5% of the prison population was homeless.

Factors behind punishment behaviour:

This next section will be focusing on the different factors that can result in a person's punishment behaviour.

For example, are they for or against the death penalty?

Social factors:

As always social factors will play a role in behaviour and here are a few social factors that can make someone more punitive.

In other words, make a person more willing to support the harsher sentences.

Older people are more likely to be punitive than younger people (Hough & Moron, 1985)

Men are more punitive than women and express less confidence in the Criminal Justice System. (Hugh et al, 1988)

People with low education level have poor knowledge about the Criminal Justice System. (Mattison, Mirrlees and Black, 2000)

Overall, there are a few social factors that can impact someone's behaviour towards the criminal Justice System and punishment.

What is the Criminal Justice System's purpose?

In large part, justice and the Criminal Justice System is about retribution.

This makes sense at a very basic level, many of us want that offender to suffer and pay for the crimes they committed.

One example is that if someone

attacked one of my friends then I would want them to pay for the suffering that they have caused.

If a Criminal Justice System is perceived as too lenient than people will respond. To right this perceived wrong.

<u>Different Groups and the Criminal Justice System</u>:

Regardless of group membership; the group you are a member of; you will all have different thoughts, beliefs and values on the Criminal Justice System. Hence, here are some factors and experiences from other groups:

- Ethnicity- black people are more likely to find the Criminal Justice System discriminatory.

This is a sad truth that racism is still at large and in the USA. There are constantly issues of racism.

- Religion- Muslims and Hindus are more likely than Christians or Buddhists to believe that the police are doing a good job.

Personally, I found this fact to be interesting because I didn't actually expect Muslims to rate the UK police as doing a good job. Considering how sadly some parts of the country still think of Muslims and foreigners. Granted it is only the minority.

- Highly religious people or fundamentalists are more likely to be punitive. (Grasnick et al, 1992)

I've seen this fact being used a lot on crime programmes and for once the crime programmes are correct.

- People who believe in a just world are more likely to endorse punitive punishment. (Finamore et al,

1987; Palazinski and Shortland, 2016)

The Just World Hypothesis is a cognitive bias where people believe in an external cosmic justice or force as well as they believe that the consequences should fit the offender. Therefore, it's reasonable that they would believe in punitive punishments as they want the consequence to fit with the offender's action.

- People with highly conservative beliefs favour punitive sentences. (Baron and Hartnagel, 1996)

Thinking about this fact, this does make sense Boris Johnson's conservative manifesto in the United Kingdom December 2019 elections because I saw one of his policies that were: to have tougher sentences on criminals.

After reading the fact above, it makes

sense why he did that as he probably knew that conservatives would support and be attracted to that manifesto pledge.

Of course, he was enhancing the public's fear of crime as well.

Reactions to specific offences:

Thankfully, humans don't have one standard rule for punishment. Resulting in a lot of grey areas. This is positive because without grey areas that many people would be subjected to extreme punishment. As shown in the history of punishment section above.

One example of these differences is that Americans don't believe in the death penalty for juveniles.

Yet another example is that people favour prison sciences for violent and sexual offenders but not pretty theft.

Confidence in the Criminal Justice System:

Building upon what we discussed in a previous Chapter, Morri (2000) did a very interesting study that showed that 75% people have confidence in Criminal Justice System as they respect rights and gives people fair treatment.

However, only 25% of the public have confidence in the Criminal Justice System for being effective in crime reduction.

Personally, I find this interesting because it truly demonstrates how limited the public's knowledge is when it comes to the Criminal Justice System.

Public attitude towards Imprisonment:

The public tends to have two views when it comes to offenders.

Firstly, a lot of research has shown support for rehabilitation.

Though, there is a strong public desire to punish offenders.

It could be these paradoxical views present the greatest challenge for violent offenders.

What should happen when someone goes to prison?

The ideal version of what happens and what happens is always going to differ because the theory is more difficult to put into practice sometimes.

A common example is politics as there is a difference between a manifesto and what the politicians actually do.

The same applies to prisons.

Ideally when someone goes to prison what should happen is that they are inducted into the prison community where rehabilitation work happens including work to give them skills to make them more employable in the real world as well as they should receive an education for the same reason.

After that, there should be a resettlement period where the offender interacts with the community.

I think that this is a great idea to have because this is a proven way to help offender not to re-offend, but this is expensive.

Below are some country's re-offending rates that clearly demonstrate that this ideal isn't happening.

In the USA and the UK, 52% of offenders re-offend.

In Ireland 63% of offenders re-offend.

In Japan 43% of people re-offend.

In Norway only 20% of offenders re-offend.

Interestingly, when I was taught this topic at university the lecturer showed us a video of a Norwegian 'prison' that is this ideal incarnated because the prisoners have everything that non-prisoners have and more.

It's about the cognitive skills programmes, learn techniques for the improvements of problem-solving relevant.

Basically, shifting the criminal mindset by making them a part of a community.

Yet I think that this idea could be interesting in the future as this type of prison were offenders can get an education, do sports and get life skills in an atypical prison environment could make them less likely to offend in the future.

Nonetheless, this prison has only been going for a few years so it's likely going to be decades until we know the effectiveness of this style of prison.

It's good to think about though.

Overcrowding:

Overcrowding in prison isn't new or rare because in September 2011 63% of prison establishments were overcrowded. As cells that were for 1 person in 2006 now had 2 people in it.

Furthermore, this overcrowding is likely to lead to prison violence as from 1990-2001 there were 26 prison murders and of those murders, 11 of them were committed cellmates.

One reason for this violence caused by

overcrowding is that crowding causes both psychological and physiological stress. Meaning that offenders are more aggressive or more likely to be violent.

Imagine how you would feel if you were in a locked room made for 1 person, but you had another 3 people inside.

Although, the major problem with overcrowding is that anecdotal evidence that connects overcrowding to re-offended.

Whilst there are always problems with anecdotal evidence, it is important not to completely dismiss it as it could be 'true' or at least play a role in re-offending. Meaning if society wants to tackle re-offending completely then we would have to look at the overcrowding issue as well.

CHAPTER 19: EFFECTS OF IMPRISONMENT

Throughout this chapter, we have looked at a grand amount of effects that imprisonment can have on a person. Yet this study shows us the way how imprisonment can affect a person on an individual level. That some of the other discussed effects don't show.

Toch (1977) found eight central environmental concerns that affect prisoners greatly.

These include:

- The prisoner's loss of privacy as everything they do is monitored and they don't have their own space anymore.
- There is a safety issue in prison. One example of this issue is the threat of being attacked by a prison gang.
- The prison community's structured is an issue as it's a hierarchy and people need to adapt.
- The prisoner has less freedom which they will struggle to come to terms with.
- Their support network will be very different. That's considering that the prison has a network at all.

Another effect of imprisonment is to do with depression and stress.

Wooldroge (1999) found four concepts related to the effects of imprisonment.

These were fragility, support, activities and social stimulation.

As a result of in prison, you tend to do no or little activity and there is a lack of social simulation compared to the outside world.

As in the outside world, we might go out for dinner, phone a friend or drive to a friend's house to see them. The offenders can't do any of those things.

Why is re-offending high?

Like with all things, there is no one answer but two big reasons behind the high re-offending rate are the overcrowding of prisons as this increases stress and violence as previously mentioned.

However, the political climate plays a massive role in re-offending rates for various reasons. Like: a governmental policy increases the development gap in an area, so one area is worsened off. Then this policy could be the cause of re-offending as the people in this area have to start stealing to survive.

The most important things to remember is that there are many reasons why re-offending happens, so it's important not to try and reduce a problem down to a single cause.

CHAPTER 20: APPROACHES TO PUNISHMENT

Overall, there are three main approaches that people can take when punishing a person.

<u>Humanitarian approach:</u>

This approach focuses on humane punishments as it states that crimes aren't black and white as well as given other factors, it can be argued that in a humane society offenders deserve more rehabilitation efforts. (Crow, 2001)

I know what you're thinking- "what! We need to punish these offenders for their crimes!"

Whilst, I was never a punitive person. I do agree with you.

Personally, I think some form of

punishment is still needed.

Nonetheless, rehabilitation and treatment work in terms of reducing crime and surely that is the main part of prison.

Therefore, if we rehabilitate these offenders so they don't offend again, then surely this is better than simply throwing them into prison? Where they will not be treated, and they are extremely likely to re-offend causing further harm to society.

Going further into the rehabilitation focus, prisons can be community therapy as they get offenders to act in a community, so when they return to a real-world community. They appreciate and know how to function better within it.

In addition, once they're released they

will be more likely to take to wider society.

Additionally, a therapeutic institution has the following features: (Woodward, 2009)

- Ongoing evaluation
- Responsivity to residence's needs
- Ongoing monitoring
- Skills oriented
- Sufficient dosage of treatment
- Target criminogenic factors
- Through care

All these features make sense as without them it makes treatment and the offender's therapy a lot more difficult to be effective.

However, this therapeutic community wasn't based on research evidence. This is ideologically driven.

Rapoport (1960) provided the following

list of features that form the basis of therapeutic prisons:

- All aspects of decision making are democratised and prisoner involved.
- General permissiveness in regard to pathological behaviour that could be a problem in other contexts.
- Day to day living as part of a community.
- Development progress and change are driven by the interpersonal forces within a community.

Personally, I like the features above as I believe that if a prison community did have these features then prisoners would be more likely to become an active member of the prison community, and potentially benefit a more lot.

Furthermore, they're more likely to become more engaged with treatment programmes. Thus, decreasing the chance of re-offending.

Retribution:

This is another approach to punishment that you can take as it's an extreme approach where it's an eye for an eye.

Consequently, if you kill someone then you die.

If you rape someone then you get raped or your manhood or ladyhood gets cut off.

Personally, whilst this approach sounds, in theory, to be perfect. In reality, I don't like this approach as it's extreme, it's unethical and it doesn't work!

Utilitarian:

This approach can be referred to as deterrence because the aim of this approach is to deter others from committing crimes.

The focuses of this type of punishment are:

- Educating people- this is where we need to teach people about the consequences of committing crimes.
- Climate danger- this is where you teach others would the society that they live in does not tolerate crime.
- Deterrence- this is where you deter others from committing crimes. For example, the public hangings in the United Kingdom's history are an example of this deterrence.

- <u>What can Forensic Psychologists do for punishment?</u>

- Overall, there is no or little role for psychology in the punishment of prisoners.

- Although, the utilitarian and humanitarian approaches may use psychology to help produce changes in the offender that decreases offending behaviour.

- However, there are many roles for psychologists within the prison system from training programmes to involvement in decision making to releasing prisoners. Furthermore, there's a wide range of psychological techniques that are used in the prison system. For example psychological measuring to delivering treatment to psychological treatments. Like: Cognitive Behavioural Therapy.

- There's every reason to believe that prison whilst limited can have a significant impact on future crime.
- Meta-analysis suggests that educational programmes could be the most important to help return offenders to a crime-free life.

CHAPTER 21: VIOLENCE IN PRISON

Violence in prison isn't new or rare, but what causes the violence to happen in prison and why does it happen?

That's the focus of this next section.

In the UK, from 2006-2016 the number of murders in prisons averaged less than 3 a year so it's rare. (Inquest, 2017) But in the USA it's about 10 times higher. (Gordon, Oyebode and Minne, 1997)

To explain why prison violence happens there are two main theories according to Lahm (2008)

Firstly, there is depression theory that states prison violence occurs because of the degrading and stigmatizing conditions of the prison. Leading to offenders acting out violently in response to these conditions because they reply on the prison conduct code of violence.

This theory provides an environmental explanation that blames the prison for the behaviour.

Personally, I think this theory is good because it demonstrates how the poor conditions that some prisoners face can lead to violence.

On the other hand, it's a reductionist theory meaning that the theory only focuses on one cause and ignores other causes. Such as cognitive and biological causes.

Importation theory:

This theory is a bit more interesting because the theory states that prison is an open system.

Therefore, prison violence is a result of attitudes, values and motivations from outside the prison system moving into it. Especially, as the adaption to prisons life is shaped by the offender's prior experience and socialisations.

In other words, this theory means that the attitudes, beliefs and values of the offender influence the behaviour of the offenders inside the prison.

For example: if you had a bunch of murders come into the prison that valued violence and had a very extreme honour code, then over time these values will affect the prison environment. Resulting in violence as these murders seek to enforce their values.

Both theories:

As always, I believe that these two

theories are correct in their own ways because bad conditions do lead to violence. For example:

people fight for food when their bad conditions require them to fight.

Equally, the prison community is shaped by its member's attitudes, values and beliefs.

According to a survey done by Lahn (2008) at 30 prisons in the US. He found that the results supported both theories and that both theories aren't exclusive of each other.

Basically, the theories work together to explain prison violence.

<u>Is prison safer than the outside world?</u>

The answer to that question depends on the cause of death you're looking at because death due to illness and homicide are significantly lower in prisons than the outside world.

On the other hand, deaths due to suicide were significantly higher in prison.

Overall, there is no simple answer to that question.

CHAPTER 22: SUICIDE AND SELF-HARM IN PRISON

Suicide and Self-harm in prisons:

Suicide and self-harm are horrific concepts yet in terms of psychology it's very interesting because we are hard-wired to survive, so why would we want to stop this survival instinct?

Yet that's a concept for another day.

Internationally, the leading cause of deaths in prisons is suicides. (WHO, 2007) and prison suicide rates are between 3 to 6 times higher than the population's rate. (Fazel, Gramn, King and Hauton, 2011)

In addition, there are 22 times more attempted suicides and suicidal thoughts compared to successful suicides. (Tartaro and Runddel, 2006)

In the UK, there were 7,000 incidents of self-harm and this goes against the idea that no harm will come to you in prison.

Although, whilst the number of self-harm incidents were high. The number of suicides is decreasing from 93 suicides in 2003 to 58 in 2010.

Finally, most suicides in prison occur in the first week and 50% of all suicides happen in the first month.

The UK average suicide rate in prisons is about 2 per week.

Thus, I hope that we can all clearly see that suicide is a massive problem in prisons.

Reasons for suicides:

While this topic will be dotted through this larger section about suicide. One cause of suicide is that sometimes suicide follows quickly after committing a violent crime as Flynn et al (2009) discovered serval trends- as well as suicidal men usually kill their spouse or partner whereas women kill their children.

Furthermore, people who commit suicide in prison use a wide range of methods. For instance:

- 23% used sharp objects.
- 42% of people died the same day as the murder.
- 75% killed themselves with 3 days.

Consequently, these findings suggest that prison isn't the primary factor for prison suicide.

How can we prevent suicides in prison?

Towl (1996) suggested a few strategies to help monitor and prevent suicides:

- Reduce the number of remanded prisoners and those with mental health problems

This would be helpful as remanded prisoners; I'll explain more in a minute; don't see a future as they will be returned to lower courts. This lack of a future increases the likelihood of suicide.

The same goes for people with mental health problems.

- Try to decrease consequences for reporting as this may lead to an increase in reporting.

This would lead to those suicidal people getting the help they would need to prevent them from committing suicide.

- Enable staff to identify and assist prisoners with suicidal thoughts.

Again, this would allow suicidal people to get the right help that they would need in order to not be suicidal.

Lastly, Bukstel & Kilman (1980) conducted a meta-analysis of 90 studies and they found passive and dependent people tend to adjust well to prisons as well as indeterminate sentencing leads to adjustment problem.

This makes sense as if you don't know how long you're going to be in prison for then you don't know if it's worth making 'friends' or becoming a part of the community. It means that you have the hope of being out soon as well.

Nonetheless, this connects to suicide because indeterminate sentencing leads to the offender seeing no future. Making

them more likely to commit suicide as a
result.

CHAPTER 23: MENTAL HEALTH AND CRIME

Mental illness and crime is a very interesting topic because if you watch the media or TV programmes then they always mention mental illness is related to crime.

But what is the truth?

That is the aim of this chapter as we scratch the surface of this modern topic.

Overall, there seems to be little doubt that certain types of mental disorders do in fact increase the likelihood of violence.

However, it is difficult to say who is at risk and who amongst the mentally ill are likely to be the most violent.

We'll explore the reason why in a moment, but this is because other factors can increase the likelihood of violence as well as the mental illness.

What other factors increase the likelihood of violence?

Several other factors in addition to the mental illness itself tend to have a greater effect on the mentally ill. Including substance abuse and alcohol.

Although, this is because there's fewer of them.

Putting this fact into an easy to understand example, let's say that 100,000 clinically normal people were tested and 30,000 of them were discovered to be substance abusers.

That means that 30% of those people were substance abusers.

Subsequently, let's say that 50,000 mentally ill people were tested; so there are 50,000 LESS people in this group, and the study found that 30,000 people in this group were substance abusers.

Meaning that 60% of this fictional mentally ill group were substance abusers.

Overall, showing you that merely as a result of there being less mentally ill people in the world. People can make grand claims that certain things affect the mentally ill more than clinically normal people.

This highlights the need for good research to prove that these claims are based on facts and not unfair prejudice.

What is the relationship between mental illness and crime?

In reality, the relationship between crime as well as mental illness is small and the public is more at risk from young men and substance abusers than the much rare schizophrenics.

Why is there is link associating mental illness with crime?

Personally, I blame the media and television because the media always focuses on the most sensational of crime (as discussed previously) and sometimes these are linked to mental health.

Nonetheless, this is a difficult question to answer so let's explore in this topic further.

Firstly, it is too reductionist; where you try to narrow the reason down to one singular cause like stating depression is caused by genetics. Whilst ignoring the cognitive and sociocultural reasons; to say that mental illness causes crime.

Please see Abnormal Psychology for more information

Especially, when other factors are involved. Such as drugs used to treat the mentally ill can cause an increase in aggression.

Leading to a possible increase in violent crime and this wouldn't be the fault of the mentally ill. As the fault would lie in the drugs as they caused aggression to increase.

Furthermore, it could be society's fault that a link is perceived to exist. As changes in social policy; a governmental policy that affects people; can possibly lead to an increase in these perceived relationships.

For example: if there's a change in social policy that states that community-based rehabilitation is better. Leading to the mentally ill being out of prison. This could increase the risk to the public as there could be more opportunity for the mentally ill to commit crimes.

Although, it MUST be noted that society has an amazing ability to generalise the actions of a few to an entire subgroup of individuals.

Thus, it is not a strange or unreasonable idea to propose that humanity stereotypes the mentally ill as criminals just because a hand of mentally ill people in the past have committed crimes.

This stereotyping; which can be read in more detail in my book Sociocultural

Psychology; isn't new as the following are all examples of where humanity has stereotyped other groups due to the actions of a few:

- All Muslims are terrorists due to the actions of a few extremists.
- All rapists are homosexual when it's very few and in fact, more heterosexuals are rapists, as previously discussed.
- And there are many more examples.

Overall, this shows how stereotyping can be applied to minorities by the dreadful actions of a few misguided souls.

Please note rehabilitation in the community is still important in the treatment of offenders.

In addition, the risk factors that can predict violent behaviour is becoming increasingly understood.

For example, as well as the types of diagnosis, whether the anti-social behaviour started in childhood or later, hallucinations or delusions can all predict violence.

<u>Mental Illness and Courts:</u>

Now it's time to enter an interesting topic as I think one of the many reasons why mental illness, as well as crime, is associated together is because of the perceived overuse of the insanity defence.

For instance, I once remember that my mother mentioned that mental illness is rubbish because it's always what criminals try and use to defend themselves.

Now, this... misguided opinion can be broken down into a few different components that reveal more about the general human population.

Firstly, people believe that the insanity or another mental illness defence is used a lot more than it actually is as it's only used when there's probable cause or when certain legal criteria are met.

One possible reason for this could be because humans have another great ability to only memory interesting pieces of information.

Therefore, people are more likely to remember a murder case involving an insanity defence as that is less often compared to your standard boring murder trial with a clinically normal person.

Secondly and this fact I find truly heart-breaking as a person who wants to support the mentally ill now and, in the future, but when a false claim is made about mental illness causing the crime and the offender doesn't have a mental illness. This casts down on all the real cases were mental illness can legitimately be used as a defence.

I know that that was confusing, so I'll take the same concept and put it in a different context.

Let's use rape as an example.

Sadly, some people lie about being raped for various reasons and when the lie is discovered. This ultimately impacts the public's confidence so when someone who has been raped comes along.

The public automatically think 'have they been rape or are they just trying to get attention like X was?'

Meaning that society is more suspicion

and most probably less likely to prosecute or take this real case seriously. As a result of one person's lies.

Overall, I hope that this shows you how lying can impact the Criminal Justice System.

The Psychology of Mental Illness and Courts:

Diving into the theory behind this new topic mental illness plays a massive role in courts. This is because legal concepts like competence, fitness to stand trial and diminished responsible have been around for centuries.

However, the problem with these mental legal concepts is that they are not simple to equate to psychological variables as well as there aren't the same in different jurisdictions.

In other words, it's difficult to make an

internationally recognised definition of these difficult legal concepts as each country has its own definition.

For instance: in the UK the considerations involved in fitness to stand trial involves:

- Having the ability to understand the evidence
- The ability to follow court proceedings
- Being able to understand that jurors can be objected and challenged
- The ability to instruct lawyers effectively
- Being able to understand the implication and meaning of the charges against them. (Grubin, 1996a)

Whereas, the US system can be simplified defined as the ability to understand and consult with a lawyer at that moment.

On the whole, I hope that you have found this interesting and enlightening.

BIBLIOGRAPHY:

Howitt, D. (2018). Introduction to forensic and criminal psychology. Essex, UK: Pearson. 6th edition.

Brown, J., Shell, Y. & Cole, T. (2015). Forensic Psychology: Theory, research, policy and practice. 1st edition

Wood, J. & Gannon, T.A. (2009). Public opinion and criminal justice. Devon, UK: Willan Publishing.

**GET FOR FREE
WHEN YOU
CLICK THE LINK
BELOW!**

HTTPS://WWW.SUBSCRIBEPAGE.
COM/N9V0D5

Thank you for reading.

I hoped you enjoyed it.

If you did, please consider leaving an honest review as this helps with the discoverability of the book and I very much appreciate it.

If you want a FREE book and keep up to date about new books and project. Then please sign up for my newsletter at www.connorwhiteley.net/

Have a great day.

About the author:

Hello, I'm Connor Whiteley, I am an 18-year-old who loves to write creatively, and I wrote my Brownsea trilogy when I was 14 years old after I went to Brownsea Island on a scout camp. At the camp, I started to think about how all the broken tiles and pottery got there and somehow a trilogy got created.

Moreover, I love writing fantasy and sci-fi novels because you're only limited by your imagination.

In addition, I'm was an Explorer Scout and I love camping, sailing and other outdoor activities as well as cooking.

Furthermore, I do quite a bit of charity work as well. For example: in early 2018 I was a part of a youth panel which was involved in creating a report with research to try and get government funding for organised youth groups and through this panel. I was invited to Prince Charles' 70th birthday party and how some of us got in the royal photograph.

Finally, I am going to university and I hope to get my doctorate in clinical psychology in a few years.

Please follow me on:

Facebook: https://www.facebook.com/connor.whiteley.3150

Website: www.connorwhiteley.net

Twitter: @whiteleyscifi

Please sign up for my newsletter on my

website for two free short stories!

Please become one of my Patrons for many monthly rewards at:

https://www.patreon.com/Connorwhiteley

Please leave on honest review as this helps with the discoverability of the book and I truly appreciate it.

Thank you for reading. I hope you've enjoyed.

Want a great new read?

The Angel of Freedom

Book 2 in the Brownsea Series

When the team is dispatched to infiltrate one of Nemiel's forges; where child labour as well as death is thriving; they soon learn that this is their chance to light the fire of rebellion against Nemiel once and for all. However, can they success when Nemesis comes to the forge to unleash his vengeance upon Kieron?

Want a great book and a deal?

Garro: Collection

Ebook- 3 novels for the price of 2 and 22 FREE short stories.

Follow Garro's story from the fight to save the Galaxy from Galaxy's End to the battlefields of Hiuidium and an unthinkable alliance with the Iarannthans to the ultimate battle to save humanity when earth is besieged on all front.

Garro is surrounded by amazing heroes but will they all survive the trilogy?

testing- ethics and psychology

A guide to mental health and treatment around the world- A Global look at depression

Forensic Psychology

Other books by Connor Whiteley:

The Angel of Return

The Angel of Freedom

Garro: Galaxy's End

Garro: Rise of the Order

Garro: End Times

Garro: Short Stories

Garro: Collection

Companion guides:

Biological Psychology

Cognitive Psychology

Sociocultural Psychology

Abnormal Psychology

Psychology of Human Relationships

Health Psychology

Developmental Psychology

Research in Psychology

Audiobooks by Connor Whiteley:

Biological Psychology

Cognitive Psychology

Sociocultural Psychology

Abnormal Psychology

Psychology of Human Relationships

Health Psychology

Developmental Psychology

Research in Psychology

Garro: Galaxy's End

Garro: Rise of The Order

Garro: Short Stories

Business books:

Time Management: A Guide for Students and Workers

Leadership: What Makes a Good Leader? A Guide for Students and Workers.

Business Skills: How to Survive the Business World? A Guide for Students, Employees and Employers.

Business Collection

GET YOUR FREE BOOK AT:
WWW.CONNORWHITELEY.NET

Printed in Great Britain
by Amazon

41184449R00177